25x ARTICLES | 25x GUIDED NOTE SETS
25x HIGH-LEVEL REFLECTION QUESTION SETS
25x HYPOTHETICAL SETS | 25x VOCABULARY SETS
25x CROSSWORDS | 25x WORD SEARCHES

25x

25x: U.S. History - Part 1

Foundations to Reconstruction

3andB Inc. | Pocatello, Idaho

version 1.0 - October 1, 2024

For more information: 3andB.com | email: info@3andB.com

Welcome & Instructions

Welcome to 3andB's ***25x: U.S. History - Part 1*** workbook. Our workbook is an ideal resource for parents and educators who are looking to introduce students to important concepts and terminology related to U.S. History.

As a parent or teacher, we suggest reviewing and familiarizing yourself with the workbook content to facilitate a more engaging learning experience. We recommend assigning a designated time each week for the student to complete the assigned reading, guided notes, reflection questions, and term definitions, followed by word search and crossword activities.

Our workbook is strategically structured with 25+ topics that offer a comprehensive overview of important U.S. History concepts, terminology, and best practices. Each section includes a short and engaging article followed by guided notes and thought-provoking reflection questions, allowing students to internalize the material and apply it to their daily lives.

To enhance the learning experience, we suggest discussing the concepts with the students and encouraging them to brainstorm real-life scenarios where they can apply the concepts learned. This approach brings theoretical concepts to life, leading to a more meaningful and engaging experience for the students.

The workbook also includes 10 terms per section that the students are encouraged to define. We recommend that educators reinforce the importance of finding the best answer when defining these terms, as it will aid the students in understanding and internalizing the concepts.

As a career-oriented and professional organization, 3andB recognizes the importance of a high-quality education that prepares students for future success. Our workbook seeks to introduce U.S. History concepts that empower students to navigate real-life situations with confidence and a greater understanding of their capabilities.

Finally, we encourage feedback from our users to better understand how we can improve our products and services. Thank you for choosing 3andB's ***25x: U.S. History - Part 1*** workbook. We believe our workbook offers a great foundation for a fulfilling, successful future for our youth.

Very truly yours,
The 3andB Team

TABLE OF CONTENTS
25x: U.S. History - Part 1
Foundations to Reconstruction

1. Introduction to US History and Its Importance

by 3andB Staff Writer | October 1, 2024

Unlocking America's Past: Why US History Matters to You

Have you ever wondered how the United States became the nation it is today? Imagine stepping into a time machine and witnessing the pivotal moments that shaped our country. That's exactly what studying US history allows you to do! From the arrival of the first Indigenous peoples thousands of years ago to the fast-paced digital age we live in now, American history is a fascinating journey through time that directly impacts your life today.

US history is more than just a collection of dates and names. It's a complex tapestry of human experiences, triumphs, and challenges that have molded the society we live in. By understanding this history, you gain valuable insights into the foundations of our government, the evolution of our culture, and the ongoing struggles for equality and justice that continue to shape our nation.

Let's explore why studying US history is not just important but exciting and relevant to your life. We'll dive into the key reasons for learning about our past, examine how history shapes our present, and discover how it can guide our future.

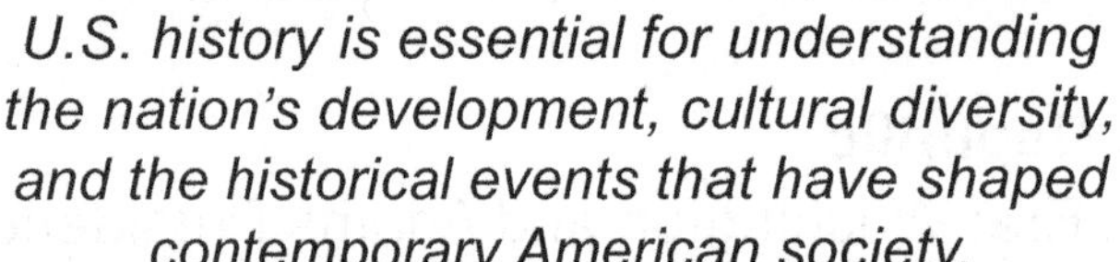

U.S. history is essential for understanding the nation's development, cultural diversity, and the historical events that have shaped contemporary American society.

Why US History Matters: Connecting Past and Present

Think of US history as the DNA of our nation. Just as your genetic code influences who you are, the events, ideas, and people of the past have profoundly shaped America's identity. The principles outlined in the Declaration of Independence and the Constitution continue to guide our government and society. By studying these foundational documents and the context in which they were created, you'll better understand the values and ideals that our nation strives to uphold.

For example, the concept of "checks and balances" in our government didn't appear out of thin air. It was a response to the founding fathers' experiences with monarchy and their desire to prevent any one branch of government from becoming too powerful. Understanding this history helps you appreciate why our government is structured the way it is and why protecting these systems is crucial for maintaining democracy.

Navigating the Present

US history isn't just about the past—it's a roadmap for understanding the present. Many of today's headlines have roots in historical events and ongoing societal issues. Take the civil rights movement of the 1960s, for instance. While significant progress has been made, many of the challenges and debates from that era continue today in movements like Black Lives Matter. By studying the historical context of these issues, you'll be better equipped to understand and engage with current events and social discussions.

Learning from the Past

As the saying goes, "Those who do not learn history are doomed to repeat it." US history offers countless lessons that can guide us in facing modern challenges. For example, studying the Great Depression can provide insights into economic policies and their impacts, which is valuable knowledge in today's complex global economy. Similarly, examining past public health crises, like the 1918 influenza pandemic, can inform our responses to modern health challenges.

US History in Your Daily Life

You might be surprised to discover how much US history influences your everyday experiences. The music you listen to, the foods you eat, the languages spoken in your community—all of these have been shaped by the diverse cultures and historical events that make up America's past.

Consider this: Every time you use your smartphone, you're benefiting from technologies developed during the Space Race of the 1960s. When you exercise your right to free speech on social media, you're engaging with a principle enshrined in the First Amendment over 200 years ago. Understanding these connections makes the world around you richer and more meaningful.

Shaping the Future

As a high school student, you're not just learning about history—you're preparing to make history. The challenges and opportunities of the future will require informed, engaged citizens who understand where we've been and can envision where we need to go. Whether you're interested in politics, business, technology, or the arts, a strong foundation in US history will provide you with the context and critical thinking skills to make a positive impact on society.

Your Role in the Ongoing American Story

US history isn't just about memorizing facts and dates. It's about understanding the complex, often messy process of how our nation has evolved. It's about seeing yourself as part of an ongoing story and recognizing your power to influence the next chapter.

As you embark on your journey through US history, keep an open mind and ask questions. Engage with different perspectives and primary sources. Look for connections between past events and current issues. Most importantly, consider how you can apply the lessons of history to become an informed, active participant in shaping America's future.

The story of America is still being written, and you have the opportunity to be both a student of history and a maker of history. Are you ready to unlock the past and shape the future? Your journey through US history starts now!

1. Introduction to US History and Its Importance

GUIDED NOTES

I. Key Terms

1. Democracy: ________________________________

2. Civil Rights Movement: ________________________________

3. Constitution: ________________________________

4. First Amendment: ________________________________

5. Checks and Balances: ________________________________

II. Main Concept Overview

US history is more than just dates and names. It's a complex ______________ of human experiences, triumphs, and challenges that have ______________ the society we live in today. By understanding this history, we gain valuable insights into the foundations of our ______________, the evolution of our ______________, and the ongoing struggles for ______________ and ______________ that continue to shape our nation.

III. Matching Section

Match the following terms with their descriptions:

____ Declaration of Independence	A. Created the system of checks and balances
____ Space Race	B. First inhabitants of the Americas
____ Great Depression	C. Provides insights into economic policies
____ Indigenous peoples	D. Influenced smartphone technology
____ Founding Fathers	E. Guides government and society today

IV. True/False Questions

_____ US history only affects political discussions and has no impact on daily life.

_____ The civil rights movement of the 1960s has no connection to current social movements.

_____ Understanding US history can help us better comprehend and engage with current events.

_____ The Constitution and Declaration of Independence have little relevance in modern America.

_____ Studying past public health crises can inform our responses to modern health challenges.

V. Fill in the Table

Complete the table with examples of how US history influences different aspects of our lives:

Aspect of Life	Historical Influence	Modern Example
Technology		
Music		
Government		
Civil Rights		
Economy		

VI. Application Question

Imagine you're explaining to a younger sibling why learning US history is important. Using information from the article, write a brief paragraph explaining how understanding history can help them in their daily life and future.

____

____

____

VII. Reflection/Summary

Summarize the main reasons why studying US history is important, according to the article:

1. ______________________________

2. ______________________________

3. ______________________________

1. Introduction to US History and Its Importance - Reflection Questions

1

In what ways do you see the impact of US history in your daily life?

Reflect on your typical day - from the technology you use to the rights you exercise. Can you identify specific examples of how historical events or decisions have shaped your everyday experiences? How might your life be different if certain historical events had not occurred?

2

How might understanding US history influence your future decisions as a citizen?

Consider your future role as a voter, community member, or potential leader. How do you think your knowledge of US history will impact the choices you make? Think about how historical awareness might guide your stance on political issues or your participation in civic activities.

3

What aspect of US history do you find most relevant to your personal identity or background?

Think about your family history, cultural heritage, or personal interests. How does US history intersect with your individual story? Reflect on how learning about certain historical events or figures might have deepened your understanding of your own background or community.

1. Introduction to US History and Its Importance - Hypotheticals

Scenario 1

Scenario: Imagine that your school board is considering significantly reducing the US history curriculum, arguing that it's less relevant in today's globalized world. They propose replacing it with more technology and international studies courses.

a) How would you argue for the importance of maintaining a strong US history curriculum?
b) What specific examples from the article could you use to support your argument?
c) How might reducing US history education impact students' understanding of current events and civic participation?

Scenario 2

Scenario: You've been selected to create a short video series for social media about why US history matters to teenagers. The goal is to make history engaging and relevant to your peers.

a) What key points from the article would you emphasize in your videos?
b) How would you connect historical events to issues that teenagers care about today?
c) What creative approaches could you use to make US history more appealing to a young audience?

1. Introduction to US History and Its Importance - Vocabulary

TERM	DEFINITION
Constitution	
Democracy	
Diversity	
Equality	
Founding Fathers	

1. Introduction to US History and Its Importance - Vocabulary

TERM	DEFINITION
Freedom	
Government	
Heritage	
Indigenous	
Justice	

Introduction to US History and Its Importance

P J C D Q H V J V X A K B Y Z G P J S P M H O A
Y N V X Z R V H E R I T A G E L O N T P I N Q Q
K I S M G E F R L C Y O R M Z R E F P Q Y U J O
T A Z G T H R E P N B G I Z W S M Q T I I H Q F
Q E P Y N U E R O D W J R S W O G R U V X U G Z
Q C G R F V E T N T T K M H D Q R A B A F F L C
T V J K B T D P A F N S J X S W V T G D L S C G
F Y Q X C Y O R F Q X C U W R T A C A I C I M G
M W A M R S M J F T J G S H J X N N I V O D T P
O S F O U N D I N G F A T H E R S N R E N X D Y
Z B T M Y L W T J K Q A I F J P O L M R S X C S
L H Q P T J M Z K E V P C T B C P M P S T A U M
P U N S G W P U X X H J E N U S F D J I I R D W
V U U M Z O Q F P J L U Z A F M E I J T T X I D
W W Q X C N V E M I Z L D E L G Q W V Y U G G A
H I K D K D C E P R I N D I G E N O U S T H O J
W F C E X I V R R S E E L Y G J Z Y Q X I N H U
Z A V M E J J N X N L K B R B B Y D H M O D X J
Z D O O B R T A E U M S M R R Y B H T O N D I R
J N N C G E Y R R L M E N P Y U F K A A Q B H Y
T R S R W Y V W S L E Y N R D D K G Y G X N E Q
Y S I A K W M R J Q J I D T A K C G Q U L I Y A
Y Z Z C Q A F P N P L F H X B H W D F I C E A A
E G O Y I G Z H I S Q G V U P C X E A S U F X H

Justice
Indigenous
Heritage
Government
Freedom
Founding Fathers
Equality
Diversity
Democracy
Constitution

Introduction to US History and Its Importance

Across

6. Traditions and achievements passed down through generations

7. Original inhabitants of a place, here before colonization

8. Government by the people, for the people

9. System for controlling and making decisions for a country

10. Blueprint for America's government system

Down

1. Key figures in early American history and government (Two words)

2. The state of being equal, especially in rights and opportunities

3. Variety of cultures and backgrounds in American society

4. Fair treatment and due reward in accordance with honor, standards, or law

5. The power to act or speak without restraint

2. Native American Civilizations (pre-1492)

by 3andB Staff Writer | October 1, 2024

The Rich Tapestry of Native American Civilizations Before 1492

Imagine standing atop an ancient Mayan pyramid, gazing out over a vast city teeming with life, or walking through the bustling streets of Cahokia, a metropolis larger than London in its time. These weren't scenes from a distant land, but snapshots of the Americas before European contact. The story of Native American civilizations prior to 1492 is one of remarkable diversity, innovation, and resilience. From the frozen tundra of Alaska to the lush Amazon rainforest, indigenous peoples developed complex societies that shaped the land and left lasting legacies.
In this article, we'll explore the major civilizations, their achievements, and the rich cultural tapestry they wove across the Americas.

Pre-1492, Native American civilizations thrived across North America, exhibiting diverse cultures, advanced agricultural practices, and complex social structures.

The Diversity of Native American Cultures

When we talk about Native American civilizations, it's crucial to understand that we're not discussing a single, homogeneous group. Instead, we're looking at a vast array of distinct cultures, each with its own language, customs, and way of life. These civilizations ranged from nomadic hunter-gatherer societies to complex urban centers with sophisticated political systems.

In North America, the Iroquois Confederacy in the Northeast established a democratic system of governance that would later influence the U.S. Constitution. The Pueblo peoples of the Southwest created intricate cliff dwellings and developed advanced irrigation techniques in the desert. On the Great Plains, nations like the Lakota and Cheyenne developed a culture centered around the buffalo, which provided food, clothing, and shelter.

Further south, Mesoamerica saw the rise of several powerful civilizations. The Maya built impressive city-states, developed a complex writing system, and made significant advancements in mathematics and astronomy. The Aztecs created a vast empire in central Mexico, with Tenochtitlan, their capital, becoming one of the largest and most impressive cities in the world at that time.

In South America, the Inca Empire stretched along the Andes Mountains, connected by an extensive network of roads. They were master architects and engineers, constructing massive stone structures without the use of mortar.

Achievements and Innovations

Native American civilizations made numerous contributions to agriculture, science, and technology. One of the most significant was the domestication of crops like corn, potatoes, and tomatoes – foods that would later transform diets worldwide. The Maya developed a sophisticated understanding of astronomy, creating a highly accurate calendar system. They also invented the concept of zero independently of other world cultures.

In North America, the Haudenosaunee (Iroquois) created a political system based on consensus and shared power, which some scholars argue influenced the development of modern democracy. The Inca developed an intricate system of record-keeping called quipu, using knotted cords to track information.

Many Native American cultures also had advanced medical practices. For instance, the Aztecs performed complex surgeries and used a wide variety of medicinal plants, some of which are still used in modern medicine today.

Societal Structures and Beliefs

Native American societies ranged from egalitarian bands to hierarchical empires. Many cultures, like the Iroquois and Cherokee, were matrilineal, tracing descent through the mother's line. Others, like the Aztec and Inca, had more patriarchal structures.

Spirituality played a central role in most Native American cultures. Many believed in a deep connection between humans and nature, viewing themselves as stewards of the land rather than its owners. This worldview often led to sustainable practices that maintained ecological balance.

The Impact of 1492 and Beyond

The arrival of European explorers in 1492 marked the beginning of a profound and often tragic transformation for Native American civilizations. Diseases brought by the Europeans, against which Native Americans had no immunity, decimated populations. The subsequent centuries saw displacement, warfare, and cultural suppression that dramatically reshaped the indigenous landscape of the Americas.

However, it's crucial to remember that Native American cultures didn't simply disappear. Many adapted and persevered, maintaining their identities and traditions despite enormous challenges. Today, Native American communities continue to fight for recognition, rights, and the preservation of their rich cultural heritage.

The story of Native American civilizations before 1492 is one of incredible diversity, innovation, and resilience. From the Iroquois Confederacy to the Inca Empire, these societies developed unique solutions to the challenges of their environments, created complex political and social systems, and left a lasting impact on the world. By studying these civilizations, we gain a deeper understanding of the Americas' rich history and the diverse cultures that continue to shape our world today.

2. Native American Civilizations (pre-1492)

GUIDED NOTES

I. Key Terms

1. Iroquois Confederacy: ______________________________

2. Mesoamerica: ______________________________

3. Quipu: ______________________________

4. Matrilineal: ______________________________

5. Egalitarian: ______________________________

II. Main Concept Overview

Native American civilizations before 1492 were ________________ and ________________.

They ranged from ________________ societies to ________________ urban centers.

These civilizations made significant contributions in areas such as ________________, ________________, and ________________.

III. Matching Section

Match each civilization or culture with its corresponding achievement or characteristic:

_____ Iroquois Confederacy	A. Built impressive city-states and developed a complex writing system
_____ Maya	B. Created a vast empire with Tenochtitlan as its capital
_____ Aztec	C. Established a democratic system of governance
_____ Inca	D. Developed a culture centered around the buffalo
_____ Lakota	E. Built an extensive network of roads connecting their empire

IV. Fill in the Table

Complete the table with information about different Native American cultures and their achievements:

Culture/ Civilization	Region	Notable Achievement
Pueblo peoples		
Maya		
Central Mexico		
Inca		
Iroquois Confederacy		

V. True/False

______ Native American civilizations were all nomadic hunter-gatherer societies.
______ The Maya independently invented the concept of zero.
______ European diseases had little impact on Native American populations.
______ All Native American societies had patriarchal structures.
______ Native American cultures disappeared completely after European contact.

VI. Application Question

Describe how the worldview of many Native American cultures, which saw humans as stewards of the land, might influence approaches to modern environmental issues.

____

____

VII. Reflection/Summary

Summarize the main points of the article in your own words. How does learning about pre-1492 Native American civilizations change your understanding of American history?

____

____

____

2. Native American Civilizations (pre-1492) - Reflection Questions

1

How does learning about Native American diversity change your view of pre-Columbian America?

Consider the variety of cultures, languages, and societies mentioned in the article. How does this complexity compare to your previous understanding? Think about how this new perspective might influence your view of American history and cultural diversity today.

2

How does Native American resilience relate to your experiences of maintaining identity through change?

Despite challenges, many Native American communities preserved their traditions. Reflect on a time when you faced significant changes but tried to maintain core aspects of your identity.

3

How might viewing yourself as a "steward of the land" change your environmental practices?

Many Native American cultures saw themselves as caretakers rather than owners of the land. Reflect on your current relationship with the environment. How might adopting this mindset affect your daily habits or your views on environmental policies?

Scenario 1

What if a Native American consensus-based governance model was implemented in a major U.S. city?

Imagine that a large American city decides to overhaul its local government, adopting a system inspired by the Iroquois Confederacy's consensus-based decision-making process. This new system emphasizes community involvement and long-term thinking.

a) How might this governance model change the way city decisions are made and implemented?
b) What potential benefits and drawbacks could arise from this consensus-based approach in a modern, diverse city?
c) How could the success or failure of this experiment influence broader discussions about democratic systems in the U.S.?

Scenario 2

What if the United Nations adopted a global environmental policy inspired by the Native American concept of land stewardship?

Consider a scenario where the UN implements a worldwide environmental protection plan based on the Native American view of humans as caretakers rather than owners of the land. This policy requires all nations to consider the impact of their actions on the next seven generations.

a) How might this have changed the balance of power between Europeans and indigenous peoples?
b) In what ways could this have affected the establishment of European colonies in the Americas?
c) How might the cultural exchange between Old and New Worlds have been different?

2. Native American Civilizations (pre-1492) - Vocabulary

TERM	DEFINITION
Aztec	
Confederacy	
Domestication	
Egalitarian	
Empire	

2. Native American Civilizations (pre-1492) - Vocabulary

TERM	DEFINITION
Indigenous	
Iroquois	
Matrilineal	
Maya	
Mesoamerica	

Native American Civilizations (pre-1492)

C Z V S Q Q K B H C D Q N Q N G G E F R U V F N
V E M P I R E Y U W V D R E S L R F M R M O W P
U B T B X X P Q R M J V E K O K N A K E A K J I
F I K B R N L W R F G Y M G F Y L J W I Y P N W
Y N I N H Y U R L C U H I K P T P H H Z A R R O
J D A P E T K M M U W S L H Q D P H Q D O T K D
G I M Y M G J G N R L T G Z O O A M J K A K A Z
M G K X O Z A D Z O Z H C O Y E X F X V V D Y N
T E L A P T M L C D A R J T A Z F N Y Y K O Q S
P N S E O K U M I J B J W T Q T N Z T F R M J X
T O V P S S U V Y T U K G D Z R H Y G V X E A S
A U W Q O L U Y M L A P R C A N I M N L J S Q U
Z S W T G Q C A M B R R T W X R R L B G U T C M
T F F T L Q V O I H Q Z I J N P O L Y K T I B E
E H V C R U W I N A J S Y A K Q Q M C R A C C S
C P Q S D D Y G L F W D C S N N U J C C C A A O
F G X K K S W C M J E P X D X L O Q W E D T R A
X W S H K K G X C I W D K J C M I U N Y K I Q M
R Z I B D N E C R U B J E N P X S P M N Z O B E
M A T R I L I N E A L Y Z R B W J H E B U N R R
E N E M Y Y N L T S E U O B A W S L Y F G I U I
Z S U J O T Q Y C J O E G X Z C O F D A I S N C
B A I K C N Q J Z D E V X K V Y Y T O X Q O F A
P B M M O F X F B D T X P Y Z B X B L R G P T K

Mesoamerica
Maya
Matrilineal
Iroquois
Indigenous
Empire
Egalitarian
Domestication
Confederacy
Aztec

Native American Civilizations (pre-1492)

Across

5. The Iroquois formed this type of political alliance.

7. Cultural region from central Mexico to Central America.

9. The Inca ruled this type of vast political entity.

10. Northeastern group whose governance influenced the U.S. Constitution.

Down

1. Tracing family lineage through the mother's side.

2. Native to a particular region or environment.

3. Describing societies with equality among members.

4. The process that gave us crops like corn and potatoes.

6. Mesoamerican civilization known for advanced mathematics and writing.

8. Mesoamerican empire with a capital that rivaled European cities.

3. European Exploration of the Americas

by 3andB Staff Writer | October 1, 2024

European Exploration of the Americas: Voyages that Shaped the New World

Imagine standing on the deck of a wooden ship, the salty sea breeze in your face, as you peer into the misty horizon. What new lands and adventures await? This was the reality for the brave European explorers who set sail across the Atlantic Ocean in the 15th and 16th centuries. Their journeys would change the course of history, connecting two worlds and ushering in an era of global exploration, trade, and cultural exchange. Let's explore the fascinating story of European exploration of the Americas, examining the motivations, key figures, and lasting impacts of these historic voyages.

European exploration of the Americas, driven by the search for new trade routes and resources, began in the late 15th century and led to significant cultural exchanges and the eventual colonization of the continent.

The Age of Exploration Begins

In the late 15th century, Europe was experiencing a renaissance of knowledge, technology, and ambition. Advances in shipbuilding, navigation, and cartography made long-distance sea travel more feasible than ever before. But what drove Europeans to embark on these perilous journeys across the Atlantic?

Several factors contributed to the Age of Exploration:

1. Economic Interests: European nations sought new trade routes to Asia, hoping to bypass Middle Eastern middlemen and access valuable spices, silk, and gold directly.

2. Religious Zeal: The spread of Christianity was a significant motivation for many explorers and their royal backers.

3. Scientific Curiosity: The Renaissance sparked a desire to learn more about the world and its diverse peoples and cultures.

4. Competition: European powers vied for prestige and influence through exploration and colonization.

Key Figures in the Exploration of the Americas

Christopher Columbus: Perhaps the most famous explorer of the Americas, Christopher Columbus, an Italian sailing for Spain, embarked on his first transatlantic voyage in 1492. Though he didn't reach his intended destination of Asia, Columbus's accidental "discovery" of the Caribbean islands marked the beginning of sustained European contact with the Americas.

Amerigo Vespucci: This Italian explorer and cartographer made several voyages to the Americas between 1499 and 1504. Vespucci was among the first to recognize that the lands Columbus reached were not part of Asia but a "New World." His accounts of his journeys led to the continents being named "America" in his honor.

John Cabot: Sailing for England, the Italian-born John Cabot reached the coast of North America in 1497, likely landing in Newfoundland or Nova Scotia. His voyage established England's claim to North America and paved the way for future English colonization.

Hernán Cortés: This Spanish conquistador led the expedition that resulted in the fall of the Aztec Empire in Mexico. His conquest of Tenochtitlan in 1521 marked the beginning of Spanish colonization in mainland North America.

Impact and Legacy

The European exploration of the Americas had far-reaching consequences that continue to shape our world today:

1. Columbian Exchange: The movement of plants, animals, culture, technology, and diseases between the Old and New Worlds transformed ecosystems, diets, and populations on both sides of the Atlantic.

2. Colonial Empires: European nations established vast colonial empires in the Americas, leading to the transfer of wealth, resources, and labor across the Atlantic.

3. Indigenous Populations: The arrival of Europeans had devastating consequences for many indigenous peoples, including disease, displacement, and cultural disruption.

4. Global Trade: The exploration of the Americas led to the development of new trade routes and economic systems, laying the groundwork for early globalization.

5. Cultural Exchange: The meeting of European, African, and American cultures resulted in new forms of art, music, language, and cuisine that continue to evolve today.

Thinking Critically About Exploration

As you study European exploration of the Americas, it's essential to consider multiple perspectives. While these voyages led to significant advancements in navigation, geography, and global connections, they also resulted in the exploitation and marginalization of indigenous peoples.

How might our understanding of this period change if we had more detailed accounts from Native American perspectives? How do the legacies of exploration and colonization continue to impact societies in the Americas today?

By examining these questions, we can develop a more nuanced understanding of this pivotal period in world history. The Age of Exploration reminds us that human curiosity and ambition can lead to both remarkable achievements and profound challenges, shaping the course of history in ways that continue to resonate centuries later.

As you reflect on the European exploration of the Americas, consider how this history has influenced your own life and community. How might understanding this period help us navigate the global challenges and opportunities we face today?

3. European Exploration of the Americas

GUIDED NOTES

I. Key Terms

1. Age of Exploration: ______________________________

2. Columbian Exchange: ______________________________

3. Conquistador: ______________________________

4. Renaissance: ______________________________

5. Cartography: ______________________________

II. Main Concept Overview

The European exploration of the Americas was driven by ______________, ______________, ______________, and ______________. These voyages led to the connection of the Old and New Worlds, resulting in significant ______________, ______________, and ______________ changes.

III. Matching Section

Match each explorer with their achievement:

_____ Christopher Columbus	A. Reached the coast of North America in 1497
_____ Amerigo Vespucci	B. Led the expedition that conquered the Aztec Empire
_____ John Cabot	C. First to recognize the Americas as a "New World"
_____ Hernán Cortés	D. Sailed across the Atlantic and reached the Caribbean in 1492
_____ Ferdinand Magellan	E. Led the first expedition to circumnavigate the globe

IV. True/False

_____ The Age of Exploration began in the late 15th century.

_____ Christopher Columbus's initial goal was to find a new continent.

_____ The Columbian Exchange only involved the movement of people between continents.

_____ European exploration had no negative consequences for indigenous populations.

_____ The voyages of exploration contributed to the development of early globalization.

V. Fill in the Table

Complete the table with information about the motivations for European exploration:

Motivation	Description	Example
Economic		
Religious		
Scientific		
Political		

VI. Application Question

Imagine you are a European explorer in the late 15th century. Describe the preparations you would make for a voyage to the Americas, considering the challenges and unknowns you might face. What would be your primary goals for the expedition?

VII. Reflection/Summary

In your own words, summarize the main impacts of European exploration of the Americas. How do you think this historical period continues to influence the world today?

3. European Exploration of the Americas - Reflection Questions

1

What personal motivations might drive you to explore unknown lands if you lived during the Age of Exploration?

Reflect on the reasons mentioned in the article - economic interests, religious zeal, scientific curiosity, and competition. How do these compare to what might motivate people to explore or take risks today? Consider modern examples of exploration, such as space travel or deep-sea exploration.

2

How does European exploration of the Americas continue to influence global dynamics today?

Think about the lasting impacts of colonial empires on current international relations. Consider how the distribution of wealth and resources established during the colonial era might still affect economic disparities between nations.

3

How might indigenous perspectives change our understanding of the Age of Exploration?

Imagine the same historical events told from the viewpoint of Native American societies. What kinds of information or insights might these perspectives provide that are missing from European accounts? Consider how indigenous narratives might shed light on the ecological, social, and cultural changes.

Scenario 1

The Red Planet Colonization: What if a private company establishes the first permanent settlement on Mars by 2030?

Imagine that SpaceX successfully creates a self-sustaining colony on Mars, beating national space agencies to this milestone and establishing a strong corporate presence on another planet.

a) How might this private colonization of Mars affect future space exploration efforts by nations?
b) In what ways could this corporate Mars settlement influence the development of international space law and governance?
c) How might the exchange of resources and technology between Earth and Mars alter the course of human technological advancement?

Scenario 2

The Deep Sea Energy Revolution: What if a new clean energy source is discovered in the deep ocean, but only in the territorial waters of a few nations?

Imagine that scientists discover a revolutionary, abundant clean energy source in deep-sea hydrothermal vents. This energy source has the potential to solve global energy needs, but it's only accessible in the territorial waters of a handful of countries.

a) How might this discovery affect global efforts to combat climate change and transition to renewable energy?
b) What could be the potential impact on international maritime law and the concept of territorial waters?
c) How might this scenario influence global economic systems and power dynamics between energy-rich and energy-poor nations?

3. European Exploration of the Americas - Vocabulary

TERM	DEFINITION
Age of Exploration	
Cartography	
Colonization	
Columbian Exchange	
Conquistador	

TERM	DEFINITION
Expedition	
Navigation	
New World	
Renaissance	
Circumnavigate	

European Exploration of the Americas

```
V Z C A G E O F E X P L O R A T I O N O Q P D D
P C Y O I C A M S L U J N O E E Z H G K U Y X X
S F W Y J I N T Y N K J Z R V X Y P T Y Y X K U
I O B Q U R L G Q Z Y M K K J Y P R P K T S E M
E A W C W M U W G N K X S E E V P E X C M O W K
Z D R P L A G N E D E S X R K J R R D Q P S G A
N L M P C E N E W W O R L D V P X E Q I A Q X Q
Q U V S C J Q G S F C X Y X H F U W Q D T T P M
L D K S O Q C T J O T U Y F Q Y K O W S L I P J
B L A U L N U O K F B A K Q N A V I G A T I O N
R C V E U Y R L N M X U L O F Z V Z T F Y A S N
Z I B T M T M P O Q E S C O C V D H L K R Z W D
S R A X B W X S R J U I P O E H O T F N Y L Z M
D C I W I U Z U E Q J I H C L G P F G X N X X M
L U M D A W Q Q N G N R S J A O S B E X R K A T
B M I W N N G W A U U B F T L R N Q G P R Q P S
B N W Y E D T L I W A J L F A A T I B O I Z V I
L A I Q X J H P S R A Q I E Z D Z O Z U E Y J C
T V K S C P L E S D X K P T B H O D G A X K V V
X I O N H H R K A T R X I Y R I I R F R T B W B
C G U L A M T Z N N U I V E G Y V Y F P A I M D
Y A B X N Z R R C V U T R C O Y G N T H X P O Y
M T J M G V B D E S Y J N Q J M Y S O H H T H N
W E B J E X Y U F L U B Q H J V K H E R Y H E Y
```

Circumnavigate

Renaissance

New World

Navigation

Expedition

Conquistador

Columbian Exchange

Colonization

Cartography

Age of Exploration

European Exploration of the Americas

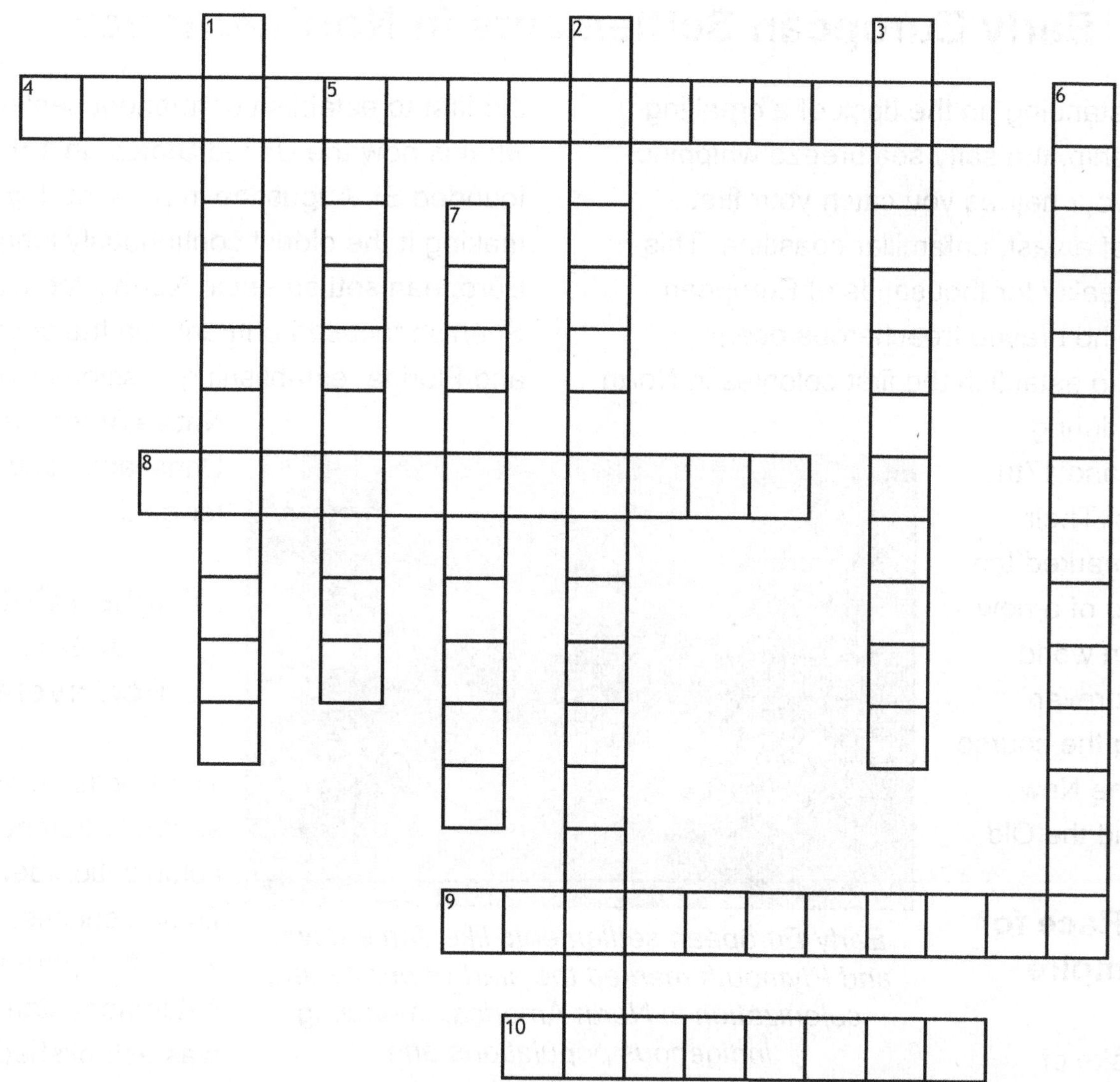

Across

4. Era of extensive overseas exploration beginning in the 15th century. (3 words)

8. The science of map-making that advanced during this period.

9. Period of cultural rebirth and scientific advancement in Europe.

10. Term used by Europeans to describe the Americas after their "discovery". (2 words)

Down

1. Process of settling and establishing control over a new area.

2. Transfer of goods, ideas, and diseases between Old and New Worlds. (2 words)

3. Spanish explorer-soldier in the Americas during the 15th-16th centuries.

5. Journey undertaken for a specific purpose, often exploration.

6. To sail all the way around something, especially the world.

7. The process of planning and directing the route of a ship or aircraft.

4. Early European Settlements in North America

by 3andB Staff Writer | October 1, 2024

Pioneering the New World: Early European Settlements in North America

Imagine standing on the deck of a creaking wooden ship, the salty sea breeze whipping through your hair as you catch your first glimpse of a vast, unfamiliar coastline. This was the reality for thousands of European settlers who braved treacherous ocean voyages to establish the first colonies in North America during the 16th and 17th centuries. Their journey marked the beginning of a new chapter in world history, forever changing the course of both the New World and the Old.

Early European settlements like Jamestown and Plymouth marked the start of permanent colonization in North America, impacting indigenous populations and the continent's development.

The Race for Empire

In the wake of Christopher Columbus's voyages, European nations scrambled to claim pieces of the New World for themselves. Spain, England, France, and the Netherlands each sought to establish footholds in North America, driven by dreams of wealth, religious freedom, and territorial expansion.

Spanish Settlements: The First Footprints

Spain, riding high on the success of its conquests in Central and South America, was the first to establish permanent settlements in what is now the United States. In 1565, they founded St. Augustine in present-day Florida, making it the oldest continuously inhabited European settlement in North America. The Spanish focused primarily on the southwest and Florida, establishing missions to convert Native Americans to Christianity and search for gold.

English Colonies: A Tale of Perseverance

The English made several attempts at colonization before finding success. Their first permanent settlement, Jamestown, was established in 1607 in Virginia. Despite a rocky start marked by disease, starvation, and conflicts with local Native American tribes, Jamestown survived and became the cornerstone of England's colonial empire in North America.

In 1620, a group of religious separatists known as the Pilgrims founded Plymouth Colony in Massachusetts. Their quest for religious freedom and self-governance laid the groundwork for future English settlements in New England.

French Explorations: Fur and Faith

The French took a different approach to colonization, focusing on the fur trade and missionary work rather than large-scale settlement. They established a presence along the St. Lawrence River, the Great Lakes, and the Mississippi River valley. Quebec City, founded in 1608, became the heart of New France and a base for further exploration of the continent's interior.

Dutch Endeavors: New Netherland

The Dutch, too, sought their piece of the New World pie. In 1624, they established New Amsterdam on Manhattan Island, which would later become New York City. The colony of New Netherland stretched from present-day Delaware to Connecticut, though it was relatively short-lived, falling to English control in 1664.

Life in the Colonies: Challenges and Triumphs

Early colonial life was far from easy. Settlers faced numerous challenges, including:

1. Harsh climate and unfamiliar terrain
2. Food shortages and disease
3. Conflicts with Native American tribes
4. Isolation from their home countries

Despite these hardships, the colonists persevered. They learned to cultivate new crops, established trade networks, and developed unique forms of government and social structures. The Mayflower Compact, signed by the Pilgrims in 1620, was an early example of self-governance in the colonies and laid the foundation for future democratic ideals.

Impact on Native American Populations

The arrival of European settlers had a profound and often devastating impact on Native American populations. Diseases brought by the Europeans, for which Native Americans had no immunity, decimated many tribes. Additionally, conflicts over land and resources led to warfare and displacement of indigenous peoples.

Legacy of Early Settlements

The early European settlements in North America set the stage for the future development of the United States and Canada. They introduced new languages, religions, and cultural practices to the continent, forever altering its landscape. The experiences and ideals of these early colonists—including concepts of self-governance, religious freedom, and economic opportunity—would later influence the formation of the United States and its foundational documents.

The story of early European settlements in North America is one of ambition, struggle, and transformation. From the sun-baked streets of St. Augustine to the frigid shores of New England, these pioneering communities laid the groundwork for the diverse and complex nations that would eventually emerge. As we study this period, we gain valuable insights into the origins of modern North American society and the enduring legacy of those early settlers who dared to dream of a new life in an unknown world.

4. Early European Settlements in North America

GUIDED NOTES

I. Key Terms

1. Colonization: ____

2. New World: ____

3. Pilgrims: ____

4. Mayflower Compact: ____

5. Indigenous peoples: ____

II. Main Concept Overview

The early European settlements in North America were established by

______________, ______________, ______________, and ______________

in the 16th and 17th centuries. These nations were driven by desires for

______________, ______________, and ______________.

III. Matching Section

Match each term with its correct description:

_____ St. Augustine	A. Oldest continuously inhabited European settlement in North America
_____ Jamestown	B. Heart of New France
_____ Plymouth Colony	C. Established by Pilgrims seeking religious freedom
_____ Quebec City	D. First permanent English settlement in North America
_____ New Amsterdam	E. Dutch settlement that later became New York City

IV. Fill in the Table

Complete the table with information about each nation's settlements and motivations:

Nation	Main Settlement Areas	Primary Motivations
Spain		
England		
France		
Netherlands		

V. True or False

_____ The Spanish were the first to establish permanent settlements in what is now the United States.

_____ The Pilgrims signed the Mayflower Compact in 1620.

_____ French colonization focused primarily on large-scale settlement rather than trade.

_____ Native American populations were unaffected by the arrival of European settlers.

_____ The early European settlements had no influence on the future development of the United States.

VI. Application Question

Imagine you are a European settler arriving in North America in the early 17th century. Describe three challenges you might face and how you would attempt to overcome them.

Challenge 1: ____

____

Challenge 2: ____

____

Challenge 3: ____

____

VII. Reflection/Summary

In your own words, summarize the main impacts of early European settlements on North America. How do you think these early colonial experiences shaped the future of the continent?

____

____

____

____

____

4. Early European Settlements in North America - Reflection Questions

1

What skills would be most crucial if you were to establish a new settlement in an unfamiliar environment today?

Think about the challenges faced by early settlers and how modern technology and knowledge might change the experience. What timeless skills remain essential?

2

In what ways do early European-Native American interactions continue to influence relationships between cultural groups in North America today?

Reflect on the long-term consequences of these early encounters and any parallels you see in modern society.

3

Considering the environmental changes brought by European settlement, how should we balance progress and preservation in our society today?

Reflect on the long-term environmental impacts of colonization and how this history might inform our current approach to development and conservation.

4. Early European Settlements in North America - Hypotheticals

Scenario 1

What if the Pilgrims had landed in Florida instead of Massachusetts?

The Mayflower, blown off course, lands near present-day Jacksonville, Florida in November 1620. The Pilgrims encounter a warmer climate, different Native American tribes, and proximity to Spanish settlements.

a) How might the warmer climate and different environment affect the Pilgrims' survival rate in their first year?
b) How could interactions with local Native American tribes differ from those in New England?
c) What potential conflicts or alliances might arise between the Pilgrims and nearby Spanish settlements?

Scenario 2

What if France had maintained control of its North American territories?

Imagine France successfully defended its North American territories during the Seven Years' War (1756-1763), maintaining control of Canada and the Louisiana Territory.

a) How might the linguistic and cultural landscape of North America be different today?
b) How could this have affected the American Revolution and the formation of the United States?
c) What implications might this have had for westward expansion and relations with Native American tribes?

4. Early European Settlements in North America - Vocabulary

TERM	DEFINITION
Colonization	
Expedition	
Frontier	
Mayflower	
Missionary	

4. Early European Settlements in North America - Vocabulary

TERM	DEFINITION
New World	
Pilgrim	
Quaker	
Settlement	
Smallpox	

Early European Settlements in North America

W J E S A J S O D T R K S S B H F J M P F C J O
E J X J E P O T I K E X W Y G M F R O N T I E R
S M P U J D P P H R I V U P K W S H I N S S G C
L V E E H P E Z O N X O Y L G M T T N F B L E P
R J D I I M C A S R E K K Q U M M Y N D A N L Z
T F I S N I O A A V E W I R U I L N Y W U K N S
Q L T B T S L P D Q C R W Q Y M C W G A H S H E
W S I I L S O E F M G K K O W Q B T F F F V C T
K P O S F I N P C J O Z Q Y R P Q F R L O T J T
M N N C H O I N K D W K W J R L I J G V S V Q L
K N H N Y N Z P Y M V C P B J G D W X V L X D E
O B S M D A A J I E V G K J C E B E I Z P F B M
I E W R U R T T S L I D R O N F M I J G K U W E
O A P G R Y I V D T G U W Q A X Z D L J M R Z N
S Q O O O U O G C V T R Z F Y E C G D B O M B T
A K U Y N Q N B F B L T I N H M C S L C L Y J M
F A X Q O D D M X R R S S M J N Q U A K E R Z K
T Q M H C S S U W E H M J L O E C H F P B A F U
W K P J I B R S N D Z A R P T M A Y F L O W E R
V R Y S N Y D C E J X L G W Y Y S O N L R C Q W
M J Y Z C X D K O R A L Y V R A D K U K V I I F
Y G Z L S L D C B E G P Y N D O K F I X Z C L K
Z S L U O W M O Y H F O Q F N C K Q K D B R N Q
O M D M X V M L Z L T X T N M T H A O W N T M T

Smallpox
Settlement
Quaker
Pilgrim
New World
Missionary
Mayflower
Frontier
Expedition
Colonization

Early European Settlements in North America

Across

5. Term used by Europeans to describe the Americas. (2 words)

6. A place where people establish a community.

8. One of the English Separatists who founded Plymouth Colony in 1620.

9. The process of settling and establishing control over a new area.

10. The ship that transported the Pilgrims to North America in 1620.

Down

1. A journey undertaken for a specific purpose, especially exploration.

2. A contagious disease that devastated Native American populations.

3. A member of the Religious Society of Friends, a Christian group.

4. The outer limit of settled land; a border region.

7. Spreading the faith, often hand-in-hand with colonization.

5. The Columbian Exchange and Its Impact

by 3andB Staff Writer | October 1, 2024

The Columbian Exchange: Reshaping Two Worlds

Imagine biting into a juicy tomato or savoring a steaming plate of pasta. Now, picture a world where these foods didn't exist in your daily life. Before 1492, that was the reality for Europeans, while people in the Americas had never tasted wheat or sugar. The Columbian Exchange, a monumental transfer of plants, animals, culture, technology, and diseases between the Old and New Worlds, forever altered the course of human history. This article will explore how this massive interchange reshaped societies on both sides of the Atlantic and continues to influence our lives today.

The Columbian Exchange facilitated the transfer of plants, animals, and diseases between the Old and New Worlds, profoundly transforming diets, economies, and populations on both sides of the Atlantic.

What Was the Columbian Exchange?

The Columbian Exchange began with Christopher Columbus's voyages to the Americas in 1492 and continued through subsequent European explorations and colonizations. This global transfer included:

1. Plants: Crops like potatoes, tomatoes, and corn traveled from the Americas to Europe, while wheat, sugar cane, and coffee made the journey in the opposite direction.

2. Animals: European livestock such as horses, cattle, and pigs were introduced to the Americas, while turkeys and guinea pigs crossed the Atlantic to Europe.

3. Diseases: European explorers unknowingly carried diseases like smallpox and measles to the Americas, devastating native populations.

4. Technology and Culture: European weapons, tools, and religious practices spread to the Americas, while Native American agricultural techniques and some cultural practices influenced European societies.

Impact on the Old World

The introduction of New World crops revolutionized European agriculture and diets. Potatoes, in particular, became a staple food that could grow in poor soil and harsh climates, leading to population growth and increased food security. Tomatoes transformed Italian cuisine, while corn (maize) and cassava provided new sources of carbohydrates.

However, the Exchange wasn't all positive. Tobacco from the Americas introduced a new addictive substance to European society, leading to health issues and social changes.

Consequences for the New World

For the Americas, the Columbian Exchange brought profound and often devastating changes. The introduction of European diseases like smallpox, measles, and influenza led to a catastrophic decline in Native American populations, who lacked immunity to these illnesses. Some estimates suggest that up to 90% of the indigenous population died due to these diseases.

On the agricultural front, European crops and livestock transformed the landscape. Horses, which had been extinct in the Americas, were reintroduced and quickly became integral to many Native American cultures, particularly on the Great Plains.

Global Economic and Ecological Changes

The Columbian Exchange kick-started the first truly global trade network. Cash crops like sugar, tobacco, and later cotton, grown on plantations in the Americas using enslaved labor, fueled European economies and led to the triangular trade system between Europe, Africa, and the Americas.

Ecologically, the exchange led to significant changes in both hemispheres. European animals like pigs and cattle, released into the Americas, altered ecosystems and competed with native species. Similarly, European weeds and pests inadvertently traveled to the New World, sometimes outcompeting native plants.

The Exchange's Legacy Today

The effects of the Columbian Exchange continue to shape our world:

1. *Global Cuisine:* Many of the foods we consider staples in various cultures are a direct result of this exchange. Italian tomato sauce, Irish potatoes, and Thai chilies all trace their origins to this period.

2. *Agricultural Practices:* The global spread of crops led to new farming techniques and dietary habits worldwide.

3. *Demographic Shifts:* The depopulation of the Americas due to disease paved the way for European colonization and the later forced migration of enslaved Africans, profoundly altering the ethnic makeup of the Americas.

4. *Ongoing Ecological Impact:* Invasive species introduced during this period continue to affect ecosystems around the world.

The Columbian Exchange was a pivotal moment in human history, connecting previously isolated continents and triggering a cascade of changes that reshaped the world. Its impacts on agriculture, demographics, ecology, and culture continue to influence our lives today, reminding us of the profound and lasting consequences of global interactions.

5. The Columbian Exchange and Its Impact

GUIDED NOTES

I. Key Terms

1. Columbian Exchange: ______________________________

2. Old World: ______________________________

3. New World: ______________________________

4. Indigenous: ______________________________

5. Cash crops: ______________________________

II. Main Concept Overview

The Columbian Exchange was a massive transfer of ______________,

______________, ______________, ______________, and ______________

between the Old and New Worlds, beginning in ______________.

III. Matching Section

Match each item with its correct description:

______ Potatoes	A. Devastated Native American populations
______ Horses	B. Transformed Italian cuisine
______ Smallpox	C. Reintroduced to the Americas
______ Tobacco	D. Led to European population growth
______ Tomatoes	E. New addictive substance in Europe

IV. Fill in the Table

Complete the table with examples from the Columbian Exchange:

From Americas to Europe	From Europe to Americas
Plants 1. ______________ 2. ______________	**Plants** 1. ______________ 2. ______________
Animals 1. ______________ 2. ______________	**Animals** 1. ______________ 2. ______________
Other 1. ______________	**Other** 1. ______________

V. True or False

______ The Columbian Exchange only affected agriculture.

______ European diseases had a devastating effect on Native American populations.

______ The exchange of crops and animals had no impact on global ecosystems.

______ The Columbian Exchange led to the first truly global trade network.

______ The effects of the Columbian Exchange are no longer visible in modern times.

VI. Application Question

Describe how the Columbian Exchange might have affected the daily life of:

a) A European farmer in the 16th century:

____

____

b) A Native American in North America:

____

____

VII. Reflection/Summary

Summarize the main impacts of the Columbian Exchange in your own words:

____

____

____

How does the Columbian Exchange continue to affect your life today?

____

____

____

5. The Columbian Exchange and Its Impact - Reflection Questions

1

How has the Columbian Exchange influenced the foods you eat on a daily basis?

Think about your favorite meals or snacks. Can you identify ingredients that originated from a different continent? How might your diet be different if the Columbian Exchange had never occurred?

2

How do you think your life would be different if you were born into the world before the Columbian Exchange?

Imagine your daily routine, the foods you eat, the animals you encounter, and the diseases you might face. How would these aspects of your life change in a pre-Columbian Exchange world?

3

How do you see the legacy of the Columbian Exchange continuing to unfold in the modern world?

Think about current global issues like climate change, biodiversity loss, or the spread of diseases. Can you draw any connections between these contemporary challenges and the historical Columbian Exchange?

Scenario 1

Suppose horses were never reintroduced to the Americas during the Columbian Exchange. It's now the mid-19th century in North America.

a) How would the absence of horses affect the lifestyle and culture of Native American tribes, particularly those on the Great Plains?
b) In what ways might westward expansion and communication in North America be impacted without horses?
c) How could warfare and trade between Native Americans and European settlers be different without horses?

Scenario 2

What if the exchange of plants during the Columbian Exchange was severely limited, with only a few species successfully transplanted between the Old and New Worlds? It's now the present day.

a) How might global cuisine be different without the widespread adoption of New World crops like tomatoes, potatoes, and corn?
b) In what ways could this limited exchange have affected global population growth and distribution?
c) How might agricultural practices and food security in different parts of the world be impacted by this limited exchange?

5. The Columbian Exchange and Its Impact - Vocabulary

TERM	DEFINITION
Columbian Exchange	
Epidemic	
Cash Crop	
Ecosystem	
Maize	

5. The Columbian Exchange and Its Impact - Vocabulary

TERM	DEFINITION
Domestication	
Biodiversity	
Globalization	
Plantation	
Triangular trade	

The Columbian Exchange

R Y Z I K V I A M A V C V M T E P G Z A T F F J

W M O D M C O L U M B I A N E X C H A N G E X V

T D A Z M E U J T H Y D P A W X N J J S M E I G

U U G M V E I F B R M A I D O G U Y N F L D P R

V N L V Z P V R G U I B Z S Z Q K K H Z V W I V

Z N O G Y E V C N Y I A P U K A P H I L U T B O

Q W B K O B I A N H N U N C Y L T D M I D I K R

Q K A E C O S Y S T E M I G R U Z D K R V S P D

M I L D G V P V C F I U C W U C B C P T B T R K

F Z I X Q R E S R Y M P V O Q L Q Q K F J D D A

O Z Z A T N V E Y V N L D B B Q A Q E U E Z S X

S V A S V P C L U D M A P N Z O D R S P S X E Y

A E T M X W O X D Z V N K D A H X N T G N O P W

A E I X J T V S Q M A T R L C H E K Z R X P I T

V O O B P U A R E P S A T J M V A G F U A D B Q

J C N U B S G Q K C U T G P V R P W K Z O D L O

Q H Q R I G L V I H Z I Q O J R M A M D M Z E H

M Q I Z F F Q W E B I O D I V E R S I T Y T T K

R Y C A S H C R O P W N C Q J D T C A K Y J H V

C U P N H F Z V M I T Y L B E C T S D N K Y Y Q

C D R W E P I D E M I C M A I Z E T A Y U C Q K

Q X X K M P T W K B O C X E W U X S W I K P V H

X K X D O M E S T I C A T I O N H O K G L R D I

C A G K D T P M V R U V B O B C G U D K K L N T

Triangular trade

Plantation

Globalization

Biodiversity

Domestication

Maize

Ecosystem

Cash crop

Epidemic

Columbian Exchange

The Columbian Exchange

Across

5. Widespread occurrence of an infectious disease.

6. Process of worldwide integration and interchange.

8. Three-way exchange between Europe, Africa, and the Americas. (2 words)

9. Native American crop, now known as corn.

10. Community of living organisms and their environment.

Down

1. Global transfer initiated by Columbus's voyages. (2 words)

2. Process of adapting wild plants or animals for human use.

3. Large farm, often using slave labor, for cash crops.

4. Variety of life in a particular habitat or ecosystem.

7. Agricultural product grown for profit, not sustenance. (2 words)

6. The Thirteen Colonies: Establishment and Differences

by 3andB Staff Writer | October 1, 2024

The Thirteen Colonies: Forging a New Nation on American Soil

Imagine stepping off a wooden ship onto unfamiliar shores, armed with little more than hope and determination. This was the reality for thousands of European settlers who established the Thirteen Colonies along the eastern coast of North America. These colonies, founded between 1607 and 1732, laid the groundwork for what would eventually become the United States of America. But how did these diverse settlements come to be, and what made each one unique? Let's embark on a journey through time to explore the establishment and differences of the Thirteen Colonies.

The thirteen colonies, established in the 17th and 18th centuries, developed unique social, economic, and political differences based on their geographic locations and governance.

The Birth of the Colonies

The story of the Thirteen Colonies begins with the ambitious goals of European nations, particularly England, to expand their influence and wealth across the Atlantic. These colonies were established in three distinct regions, each with its own characteristics and purposes:

1. New England Colonies: Massachusetts, Connecticut, Rhode Island, and New Hampshire
2. Middle Colonies: New York, Pennsylvania, New Jersey, and Delaware
3. Southern Colonies: Maryland, Virginia, North Carolina, South Carolina, and Georgia

New England Colonies: A Quest for Religious Freedom

The New England colonies were primarily settled by Puritans seeking religious freedom. In 1620, the Mayflower arrived in Massachusetts, carrying the Pilgrims who established Plymouth Colony. Over the next few decades, more settlers arrived, founding additional colonies in the region.

New England's rocky soil and harsh winters made large-scale farming difficult. Instead, the colonists turned to shipbuilding, fishing, and trade. They established small, tightly-knit communities centered around their religious beliefs, with education and self-governance playing crucial roles in their society.

Middle Colonies: America's Melting Pot

The Middle Colonies, often called the "breadbasket" of colonial America, boasted fertile soil and a moderate climate ideal for agriculture. These colonies were known for their ethnic and religious diversity, earning them the nickname "the melting pot."

New York, originally founded as New Amsterdam by the Dutch, was taken over by the English in 1664. William Penn established Pennsylvania in 1681 as a haven for Quakers, promoting religious tolerance and attracting a wide variety of European immigrants.

Southern Colonies: Agricultural Powerhouses

The Southern Colonies were characterized by their warm climate and fertile soil, perfect for large-scale agriculture. Cash crops like tobacco, rice, and indigo became the backbone of the southern economy. However, this agricultural success came at a great human cost, as the labor-intensive farming led to the widespread use of enslaved Africans.

Virginia, the first successful English colony in North America, was established in 1607 at Jamestown. As the southernmost colony, Georgia was founded in 1732 as a buffer against Spanish Florida and as a haven for debtors.

Colonial Differences: Unity in Diversity

While the Thirteen Colonies shared a common British heritage, they developed distinct characteristics that would shape their future roles in American history.

Government and Religion

The New England colonies practiced a form of self-government through town meetings and emphasized the importance of religion in daily life. The Middle Colonies, with their diverse population, tended to be more tolerant of different religions and cultures. The Southern Colonies often had a more hierarchical society, with wealthy planters wielding significant political influence.

Economy and Labor

New England's economy focused on maritime activities, small-scale farming, and early industrialization. The Middle Colonies balanced agriculture with growing urban centers like Philadelphia and New York. The Southern Colonies relied heavily on plantation agriculture and the labor of enslaved people, creating a stark contrast with the other regions.

Education and Culture

New England placed a high value on education, establishing schools and colleges like Harvard (1636). The Middle Colonies saw a blend of cultures and ideas, fostering intellectual growth. In the Southern Colonies, education was often reserved for the wealthy, with many children learning trades or working on plantations.

The Road to Revolution

As the colonies grew and prospered, they began to chafe under British rule. The diverse experiences and unique characteristics of each colony would play crucial roles in shaping their responses to British policies and, ultimately, their path to independence.

Did You Know? The colony of Georgia initially banned slavery, although this prohibition was later overturned due to economic pressures.

The story of the Thirteen Colonies is one of diversity, perseverance, and the foundations of a new nation. From the rocky shores of New England to the sultry plantations of the South, each colony contributed its unique flavor to the melting pot that would become the United States. As we reflect on this pivotal period in history, we can see how the differences and shared experiences of these colonies laid the groundwork for the complex tapestry of American society today.

6. The Thirteen Colonies: Establishment and Differences

GUIDED NOTES

I. Key Terms

1. Puritans: ______________________________

2. Cash crops: ______________________________

3. Melting pot: ______________________________

II. Main Concept Overview

The Thirteen Colonies were established between __________ and __________ along the ________________ coast of North America. These colonies were divided into three distinct regions: ________________, ________________, and ________________.

III. Matching Section

Match each term with its correct description:

_____ New England Colonies A. Known for religious tolerance and diverse population

_____ Middle Colonies B. Focused on cash crops and plantation agriculture

_____ Southern Colonies C. Emphasized religious freedom and maritime activities

_____ Jamestown D. Founded as a haven for Quakers

_____ Pennsylvania E. First successful English colony in North America

IV. Fill in the Table

Complete the table with information about each colonial region:

Region	Colonies	Main Economic Activities	Religious Characteristics
New England			
Middle			
Southern			

V. True or False

_____ The Middle Colonies were often referred to as the "breadbasket" of colonial America.

_____ The Southern Colonies had a climate unsuitable for large-scale agriculture.

_____ Education was equally prioritized across all colonial regions.

_____ The colony of Georgia initially banned slavery.

_____ The New England colonies had the most religiously diverse population.

VI. Application Question

Imagine you are a settler deciding which colonial region to move to in the early 18th century. Based on the information in the article, which region would you choose and why? Consider factors such as economic opportunities, religious freedom, and social structure in your answer.

____

____

____

____

VII. Reflection/Summary

Summarize the main differences between the three colonial regions and explain how these differences contributed to the diverse development of early American society.

____

____

____

____

6. The Thirteen Colonies: Establishment and Differences - Reflection Questions

1

How might your life be different if you were born into each of the three colonial regions (New England, Middle, and Southern)?

Consider the economic opportunities, religious environment, and social structures of each region. How would these factors have shaped your education, career prospects, and personal beliefs?

2

In what ways do you think the diverse characteristics of the Thirteen Colonies contributed to the eventual push for independence from Britain?

Think about how the different economic systems, religious beliefs, and governance structures across the colonies might have influenced their response to British policies.

3

In what ways do you see the legacy of the Thirteen Colonies in your own community or state today?

Consider aspects such as economic focus, religious influence, educational priorities, or governance structures. How have these colonial-era characteristics evolved over time in your area?

6. The Thirteen Colonies: Establishment and Differences - Hypotheticals

Scenario 1

Imagine that in 1750, a new communication system similar to social media is invented, allowing colonists to share messages and news instantly across all Thirteen Colonies.

a) How might this "colonial social media" change the spread of ideas between different colonies?
b) In what ways could this rapid communication affect the relationship between the colonies and Britain?
c) How do you think this might compare to the impact of social media on society today?

Scenario 2

Suppose that in 1700, a network of new roads is built connecting the major cities and ports in the Middle Colonies, making travel and trade much easier.

a) How might these new roads affect the economy of the Middle Colonies?
b) What changes might occur in the way people in different parts of the Middle Colonies interact with each other?
c) How could improved transportation impact the spread of ideas and information in the region?

6. The Thirteen Colonies: Establishment and Differences - Vocabulary

TERM	DEFINITION
Colonies	
Puritan	
Plantation	
Indentured Servant	
Charter	

6. The Thirteen Colonies: Establishment and Differences - Vocabulary

TERM	DEFINITION
Mercantilism	
Assembly	
Proprietary Colony	
Royal Colony	
Great Awakening	

The Thirteen Colonies

G S X L O Y G X E R I I C H P U R I T A N R Y Z
I U U D P A D L O G R Z Q X O U O S W A P E H R
B U H O R K L J T R D J E U Q I K T D D A L N A
B T W O O K K L M O J A W T N U A K I F S S R X
C X Z E P K K Z C E I C K P X V L P N N E N K Z
M X M H R G E R O I P J A S W J U L D N G B E Y
M I E L I D T P L M K L G N Z G S F E T R K Y M
L V M E E L X X O R O Y A L C O L O N Y E M P D
N J B I T M K J N L R I I R B B D E T X A U M K
U A I Q A M Y N I W I L J M Y K H K U V T M B A
N R M M R B E C E Q M W F M S N C U R I A T Q N
G P V Q Y K G R S A H G U I L Q I P E Y W R R Q
W B O U C O D J C K S V W F E S L V D C A Q L P
D D J G O G G S Z A Y S T N K X D V S D K R B V
V E T V L H K Q K G N X E D U R G N E I E Y L R
N I O L O E Z D Q O U T Z M H L D N R Z N N B U
L M M C N O U D V L O F I X B Y M V V W I J U V
W N B O Y F B E P S W H K L B L R B A H N Q H V
P A P M O N C G K J T H F N I U Y N N X G J J B
E E O H C M Q O G I S A E D X S O X T T B U I V
C F Q C H A R T E R C B G M R X M L X T H B V U
I V X R Y Y A G W F B O Q I P L A N T A T I O N
B C L S O C G P P K L O X J I M W A M S J W X G
G V N M D F L G P H L L L C G G X C Y Z L C M L

Royal colony
Proprietary colony
Great Awakening
Assembly
Mercantilism
Charter
Indentured servant
Plantation
Puritan
Colonies

The Thirteen Colonies

Across

3. Person who worked for a set number of years in exchange for passage to the colonies. (2 words)

6. Document granting permission to establish a colony.

7. Settlement under direct control of the British crown, ______ Colony

8. Large farm in the Southern Colonies, often relying on enslaved labor.

10. British-controlled settlements in North America, precursors to the United States.

Down

1. A member of this religious group sought to "purify" the Church of England.

2. Religious revival movement in the colonies during the 1730s and 1740s. (2 words)

4. Economic theory emphasizing exports over imports to increase national wealth.

5. Settlement owned and governed by an individual or group, ______ Colony

9. Elected group of colonists who made laws for their colony.

7. Colonial Society and Economy

by 3andB Staff Writer | October 1, 2024

Colonial Society and Economy: The Foundations of Early America

Imagine stepping back in time to the bustling streets of Boston in the 1750s. The air is filled with the sounds of horse-drawn carriages, the chatter of merchants, and the rhythmic pounding of a blacksmith's hammer. This vibrant scene offers a glimpse into the complex tapestry of colonial America's society and economy. How did the diverse groups of people in the colonies live, work, and interact? What economic systems shaped their daily lives and laid the groundwork for a future nation? Let's explore the fascinating world of colonial society and economy, uncovering the roots of American culture and commerce.

Colonial society and economy were characterized by agriculture, trade, and a rigid social hierarchy influenced by European traditions.

The Social Fabric of Colonial America: A Diverse Population

Colonial America was far from homogeneous. English settlers formed the majority in many colonies, but they were joined by waves of immigrants from other European nations, including Germany, Scotland, Ireland, and France. African slaves, brought against their will, contributed significantly to the colonial population and economy, especially in the southern colonies. By 1750, enslaved Africans constituted about 20% of the colonial population. Native Americans, though often displaced, also played a crucial role in shaping colonial society through trade, alliances, and conflicts.

Social Hierarchy

Colonial society was structured in a hierarchical manner, though less rigid than in Europe. At the top were wealthy landowners, merchants, and government officials. These elites often controlled vast tracts of land and held significant political power. The middle class consisted of skilled artisans, small farmers, and shopkeepers. This group was the backbone of colonial society, providing essential services and goods. At the bottom were indentured servants, who worked for a set number of years to pay off their passage to America, and enslaved Africans, who had no social mobility.

Religion and Education

Religion played a central role in colonial life, influencing social norms, politics, and education. The establishment of schools and colleges, such as Harvard in 1636, was often driven by religious motivations. The Great Awakening, a religious revival movement in the 1730s and 1740s, swept through the colonies, challenging established churches and promoting a more emotional and individualistic approach to faith. The diversity of religious beliefs, including Puritanism, Anglicanism, and Quakerism, laid the groundwork for future religious freedom.

The Colonial Economy: Foundations of American Prosperity

Agriculture: The Backbone of Colonial Life

Agriculture formed the cornerstone of the colonial economy. In the southern colonies, large plantations grew cash crops like tobacco, rice, and indigo, relying heavily on slave labor. Tobacco, in particular, was so valuable that it was sometimes used as currency. The middle colonies, often called the "breadbasket," produced wheat and other grains. New England, with its rocky soil, focused more on subsistence farming and other economic activities.

Maritime Trade and Commerce

The Atlantic Ocean was America's gateway to the world. Colonists engaged in triangular trade, exchanging goods with England, Africa, and the West Indies. This complex network of trade routes shaped the colonial economy and had far-reaching social implications. Fish, lumber, and ships from New England, agricultural products from the middle and southern colonies, and raw materials like iron were exported. In return, the colonies imported manufactured goods, slaves, and luxury items.

Early Industry and Craftsmanship

While not as developed as in England, colonial industry played a crucial role. Shipbuilding thrived in New England, with cities like Boston and Newport becoming major shipbuilding centers. Iron works emerged in the middle colonies, particularly in Pennsylvania and New Jersey. Textile production began to take root, especially in the form of household production. Skilled craftsmen, including blacksmiths, coopers, and silversmiths, were essential to colonial life and economy.

The Seeds of Revolution: Economic Tensions

The prosperity of the colonies did not go unnoticed by the British Crown. Attempts to regulate and tax colonial trade, such as the Navigation Acts and later the Stamp Act, created tensions. The Navigation Acts, which required colonial trade to be conducted on British ships and pass through British ports, were particularly resented by colonial merchants.

The economic relationship between the colonies and Britain was complex. While the colonies benefited from British protection and investment, they also chafed under restrictions that limited their economic autonomy. The British policy of mercantilism, which viewed colonies primarily as sources of raw materials and markets for manufactured goods, increasingly conflicted with the growing economic ambitions of the colonists.

These economic pressures, combined with the desire for self-governance, would eventually spark the flame of revolution. Events like the Boston Tea Party, ostensibly about taxation, were fundamentally rooted in deeper issues of economic control and representation.

Colonial society and economy laid the foundation for the United States we know today. The social diversity, economic ingenuity, and spirit of self-reliance that characterized this period would become hallmarks of American culture. As we reflect on this era, we can see how the colonial experience shaped not only the American economy but also the very identity of a nation poised for independence and growth.

The legacy of this period continues to influence American society and economy. The entrepreneurial spirit, the emphasis on trade and commerce, and the complex interplay between diverse social groups all have their roots in colonial America. Understanding this crucial period of history provides valuable insights into the forces that shaped the United States and continue to influence its development today.

7. Colonial Society and Economy

GUIDED NOTES

I. Key Terms

1. Indentured Servant: ____

2. Cash Crops: ____

3. Triangular Trade: ____

4. Mercantilism: ____

5. Navigation Acts: ____

II. Main Concept Overview: Colonial Society and Economy

Colonial America was characterized by __________________ social structures and a __________________ economy. The society was influenced by factors such as __________________, __________________, and __________________. The economy was primarily based on __________________, but also included __________________ and __________________.

III. Matching Section

Match the term with its correct description:

_____ 1. Great Awakening

_____ 2. Middle Colonies

_____ 3. New England

_____ 4. Southern Colonies

_____ 5. Artisans

A. Region known for producing grains

B. Relied heavily on slave labor

C. Religious revival movement

D. Focused on maritime activities

E. Skilled craftsmen essential to colonial economy

IV. Fill in the Table

Complete the table below with information about the colonial social hierarchy:

Social Class	Examples	Economic Role
Upper Class		
Middle Class		
Lower Class		

V. True or False

_____ 1. The colonial population was entirely homogeneous, consisting only of English settlers.

_____ 2. Religion played a central role in colonial life, influencing social norms and education.

_____ 3. Agriculture was a minor part of the colonial economy.

_____ 4. The Navigation Acts were welcomed by colonial merchants.

_____ 5. Colonial industry was as developed as that in England.

VI. Short Answer

1. Explain how the triangular trade system worked and its impact on the colonial economy.

___

___

2. Describe two ways in which religion influenced colonial society.

___

___

VII. Application Question

How did the economic tensions between the colonies and Britain contribute to the American Revolution? Provide specific examples from the article.

___

___

___

VIII. Reflection/Summary

In your own words, summarize the main points about colonial society and economy. How do you think these factors influenced the development of the United States?

___

___

___

___

7. Colonial Society and Economy - Reflection Questions

1

How do you think your life would be different if you lived in colonial America?

Consider your social status, education, and career opportunities. Think about the social hierarchy in colonial times. How might your current family background translate to colonial society? What kind of education and job prospects would you likely have?

2

Colonial America saw significant immigration from various European countries.

How does this compare to immigration patterns in the United States today? How has immigration shaped your community? Consider the reasons people immigrated to colonial America and compare them to reasons for immigration today. How has immigration affected the cultural makeup of your local area?

3

In what ways do you see the legacy of colonial economic practices in today's American economy?

Consider industries that were important in colonial times, like agriculture or maritime trade. How have these evolved? Are there any modern equivalents to mercantilism or triangular trade?

Scenario 1

You're a legislator drafting a bill to reform the U.S. education system. You want to address inequalities while promoting skills needed for the modern economy, much like how colonial education evolved to meet changing needs.

a) How do current educational inequalities compare to the educational disparities in colonial America?
b) What skills do you think are essential for today's economy, and how do these compare to the valued skills in colonial times?
c) How might you address the role of religion in public education, considering the influence of religion on colonial education and the principle of separation of church and state?

Scenario 2

As a social media influencer, you've been invited to participate in a campaign promoting civic engagement and voting rights, reminiscent of the colonial-era push for representation.

a) How do modern voting rights issues compare to the colonial-era concept of "no taxation without representation"?
b) In what ways can social media be used to promote civic engagement, and how does this modern form of communication compare to how information spread in colonial times?
c) How might you address concerns about misinformation in your campaign, and how does this relate to the spread of revolutionary ideas in colonial America?

7. Colonial Society and Economy - Vocabulary

TERM	DEFINITION
Colonies	
Diversity	
Hierarchy	
Mercantilism	
Navigation Acts	

TERM	DEFINITION
Revolution	
Slavery	
Subsistence	
Triangular trade	
Yeoman	

Colonial Society and Economy

V T M O P H C Z H L F T K I X R Z H T B H S T V
S F F N W R E V O L U T I O N H Y E P D I S H Y
L S U B S I S T F N C E W Y J Z U O R D G L Y U
Q E W Q J R O E W B S W M L E M H L B J V A P R
K U Q F M R B Z M D C R C E V I E R U C C V D X
M U Z O G W Q J C T Y E M C R T W L Q E A E O L
P Q S M W B Y O Y T E I U G Z C X N N F Y R C L
Y Q S N K H H C E N U F Z T E X A L A T A Y H S
Z X S U A Q T D O T N V W R B S T N N M G H S T
B I S R J V G U M M R V V K K C D C T Z U P T K
F N L S C I I W A G C I S S O T A T M I F T B L
Z N L A O Q A G N C Q V A C Q V V Z K C L O U E
S H J N L H B X A E A H J N Y P X O F X L I F M
G P X N O E K H F T K O W H G P Q L L H V P S Y
O V J A N R Z E F C I C R L Z U Z G T H U H Z M
P J F M I V X L M T O O B G F U L P U V V S W Q
B D H I E R A R C H Y Z N X E M D A T Y U D B X
P M D Y S X R E D N U S N A M H F N R F I O G S
U D I V E R S I T Y H Q R H C G Y U N T T Q E G
U Z U I H L C F Q N I M A Q T T Z J K P R F K J
Z H T T U R B S I J I X I U S U S G S T K A K B
Z T D M D X X N M D Y V V A V G S Q H R Y R D K
K F A U Y B C S H Z F G A I W H B P F I U Z L E
U P T R G X Q X M X B J T Y I J T L K T J T H L

Yeoman

Slavery

Mercantilism

Colonies

Triangular trade

Revolution

Hierarchy

Subsistence

Navigation Acts

Diversity

Colonial Society and Economy

Across

5. System of organizing people into different ranks or levels of importance.

8. Trading system involving three ports or regions, typically Europe, Africa, and the Americas. (2 words)

9. Early settlements established by a country or empire in a new land.

10. Economic policy aimed at increasing a nation's wealth through strict trade regulation.

Down

1. Means of supporting life at a minimum level, often through farming for personal use.

2. Forcible overthrow of a government or social order for a new system.

3. British laws controlling colonial trade to benefit the mother country. (2 words)

4. Variety of people from different backgrounds in a group or place.

6. Small independent farmer of middle-class status.

7. Practice of owning human beings as property, especially for forced labor.

by 3andB Staff Writer | October 1, 2024

The Dark Legacy: Understanding Slavery in Colonial America

Imagine stepping off a ship into a strange new world, not as an explorer or settler, but as someone stripped of their freedom, identity, and humanity. This was the reality for millions of Africans brought to the American colonies as slaves. Slavery in colonial America wasn't just a footnote in history; it was a complex system that shaped the economic, social, and moral landscape of the emerging nation. Let's explore the origins, impact, and legacy of slavery in the American colonies.

Slavery in the colonies became a foundational institution, primarily in the Southern states, where enslaved Africans were forced to work on plantations, shaping the region's economy and social structure.

The Roots of Colonial Slavery

Slavery in the American colonies didn't appear overnight. It evolved from a combination of economic needs, racial ideologies, and existing global practices. In the early 1600s, the first Africans arrived in Virginia, initially as indentured servants. However, as the demand for labor in tobacco, rice, and later cotton plantations grew, a more permanent and exploitative system emerged.

By the late 17th century, slavery had become codified into law, with racial distinctions used to justify the practice. Colonies passed laws defining slaves as property, denying them basic rights, and ensuring that slave status was inherited. This legal framework laid the groundwork for the expansion of slavery throughout the colonies.

The Economics of Slavery

Slavery became the backbone of the colonial economy, particularly in the South. Large plantations relied on slave labor to produce cash crops like tobacco, rice, and indigo. This system allowed plantation owners to amass significant wealth and power. The triangular trade between Europe, Africa, and the Americas further entrenched slavery, with each leg of the journey profiting from human bondage.

In the North, while slavery was less prevalent, many merchants and shipbuilders profited indirectly from the slave trade. This economic entanglement made slavery a issue that touched all parts of colonial society, not just the South.

Life Under Slavery

For enslaved Africans and their descendants, life in the colonies was marked by hardship, cruelty, and resistance. Slaves worked long hours in brutal conditions, facing punishment for any perceived infractions. Families could be torn apart at any time through sale. Despite these hardships, enslaved people found ways to maintain their cultures, build communities, and resist their oppression.

Resistance took many forms, from small daily acts of defiance to organized rebellions. Slaves would intentionally work slowly, damage tools, or feign illness. Some managed to escape, with a network of sympathetic individuals helping them flee to free territories in what became known as the Underground Railroad.

The Moral Debate

As slavery became more entrenched, so too did debates about its morality. Some colonists, particularly Quakers, began to question the ethics of owning other human beings. These early abolitionists argued that slavery was incompatible with Christian values and the ideals of liberty that were beginning to take shape in the colonies.

However, many colonists, even those who considered themselves enlightened, found ways to justify slavery. They used pseudo-scientific racism, economic necessity, and paternalistic arguments to defend the institution. This moral contradiction would continue to haunt the nation long after the colonial period.

Slavery's Legacy

The impact of colonial slavery extended far beyond the colonial period. It shaped the economic foundations of the United States, influenced its political structures, and created deep-rooted racial inequalities that persist to this day. The legacy of slavery can be seen in everything from wealth disparities to ongoing struggles for civil rights.

Understanding this history is crucial for making sense of contemporary issues around race, equality, and justice in America. By examining the roots of slavery in the colonial period, we can better comprehend the long-term consequences of this institution and work towards addressing its lasting impacts.

Slavery in colonial America was a complex and deeply influential system that shaped the nation's development in profound ways. Its effects rippled through time, influencing the Civil War, the civil rights movement, and ongoing debates about racial equality. By studying this difficult chapter of our history, we gain insights not only into the past but also into the challenges we continue to face as a society.

As you reflect on this dark legacy, consider how the echoes of colonial slavery still resonate today. How can understanding this history help us address current issues of inequality and injustice? The answers to these questions are not simple, but they are essential for building a more equitable future.

8. Slavery in the Colonies
GUIDED NOTES

I. Key Terms

1. Triangular Trade: ____

2. Underground Railroad: ____

3. Abolitionists: ____

4. Indentured Servants: ____

5. Cash Crops: ____

II. Main Concept Overview

Slavery in colonial America was a ____________________ system that significantly impacted the ____________________, social, and ____________________ landscape of the emerging nation. It evolved from a combination of ____________________ needs, ____________________ ideologies, and existing global practices.

III. Matching Section

Match the term with its correct description:

_____ Plantation	A. Network helping slaves escape to free territories
_____ Middle Passage	B. Large agricultural estate using slave labor
_____ Quakers	C. Religious group early to question slavery's morality
_____ Paternalism	D. Brutal journey of enslaved Africans to Americas
_____ Pseudo-scientific racism	E. Argument used to justify slavery as "caring" for slaves

IV. Timeline of Slavery in Colonial America

Fill in the blanks with the correct events:

Early 1600s: ____

Late 17th century: ____

18th century: ____

V. True or False

_____ Slavery was equally prevalent in all American colonies.

_____ All colonists supported the institution of slavery.

_____ Enslaved people passively accepted their condition without resistance.

_____ The economic impact of slavery was limited to the Southern colonies.

_____ The legacy of colonial slavery continues to influence modern American society.

VI. Fill in the Table: Forms of Resistance

Type of Resistance	Example
Daily Acts	
Organized	
Cultural	
Rebellion	

VII. Application Question

Describe how the institution of slavery in colonial America contradicted the ideals of liberty and equality that were beginning to emerge during this period. How did colonists attempt to reconcile these contradictions?

VIII. Reflection/Summary

Summarize the main points of the article in your own words. How does understanding the history of slavery in colonial America help us comprehend current issues related to race and equality in the United States?

8. Slavery in the Colonies - Reflection Questions

1

How does learning about slavery in colonial America change your perspective on the founding of the United States?

Consider the ideals of freedom and equality espoused by the Founding Fathers. How do you reconcile these principles with the reality of slavery? Think about how this knowledge might influence your view of early American history.

2

In what ways do you see the legacy of colonial slavery reflected in contemporary American society?

Reflect on current issues related to racial inequality, such as disparities in wealth, education, or criminal justice. How might these modern challenges be connected to the history of slavery in the colonies?

3

How might the United States be different today if slavery had never been established in the colonies?

Think about the economic, social, and political development of the nation. Consider both the direct impacts on African Americans and the broader effects on American culture and institutions.

Scenario 1

Imagine that in 1700, a prominent group of Quakers successfully convinced the Pennsylvania colonial government to immediately abolish slavery within its borders.

a) How might this have affected the economic development of Pennsylvania compared to other colonies?
b) What potential conflicts could this have created between Pennsylvania and neighboring colonies?
c) How might this early abolition have influenced the spread of anti-slavery sentiment in other colonies?

Scenario 2

Suppose that in 1776, as part of the Declaration of Independence, the Continental Congress had included a clause condemning slavery and calling for its gradual abolition throughout the colonies.

a) How might this have affected support for the American Revolution among different groups in the colonies?
b) What challenges might this have created in forming a unified government after independence?
c) How could this have changed the trajectory of slavery and race relations in the early United States?

8. Slavery in the Colonies - Vocabulary

TERM	DEFINITION
Abolition	
Chattel	
Codify	
Emancipation	
Manumission	

TERM	DEFINITION
Middle Passage	
Rebellion	
Segregation	
Slave codes	
Underground Railroad	

8: WORD SEARCH

Slavery in Colonial America

Q H N N W Y H W C F Y H G Z I E E E Y Z D G H N
S E M B G Q R L U Q G T Q Z X Y A W R G N F K H
F X F H S E G R E G A T I O N S W M W W B G F H
Q T F U Y K F V E A A Q G X L V F P K K O L K T
S F C F W A W V Q P I E D Y L E U X M U O G C U
L T F H P R F S S V E N H X D T S J Z W Y X D B
A I P Q T S C U M N M F W S B E Q S E P N F C X
V E A O T Y T E D W P V H C K V Z W E Q E I N S
E L F B O Z Q P P A L V J J V C B O Z W K I L N
C M I L O U N D E R G R O U N D R A I L R O A D
O X F S W L F R N D U D L N L I V N V D T H V D
D V J C Q V I V P S E E B L E K R E K B R E Z D
E C Y L O M A T K Y C U D U U T N M Y P E J I C
S H D Q W D E W I S U W H S Y C L A H H L U R M
N A W O Y I I Q Z O T A X H T L B N P A C E E A
W T E E R N A F X S N Z T R U L G C E W D R K N
M T W G M F J J Y Z K A U J X N H I N N Q E Z U
J E Z S N D P T J O L B L C J X U P L L B B W M
G L Z E U Q H U S F N W R H S X E A Z O H E E I
J O K B M O I F M A E K G R T W F T L K M L C S
N B L T D P A N R I U S T O R Y T I I P M L K S
Q P J H I L M O V V L A E V Y P Z O L I Z I E I
Z Q Q H D S C Q Z O P R I W Q Q C N H I D O X O
A M I D D L E P A S S A G E P U N E G J W N O N

Underground Railroad
Slave codes
Segregation
Rebellion
Middle Passage
Manumission
Emancipation
Codify
Chattel
Abolition

Slavery in Colonial America

Across

5. Secret network helping slaves escape to freedom. (2 words)

7. The act of setting free; a dream for many enslaved people.

8. To arrange laws systematically; what colonies did to establish slavery.

9. Legal term for enslaved people, treated as movable property.

10. Organized resistance; Stono and Nat Turner led famous ones.

Down

1. Laws defining the status of slaves and the rights of masters. (2 words)

2. The act of a slave owner freeing an enslaved person.

3. Separation based on race; a legacy of colonial slavery.

4. Treacherous ocean journey for captured Africans. (2 words)

6. Movement to end slavery.

9. The Great Awakening and Enlightenment in America

by 3andB Staff Writer | October 1, 2024

The Great Awakening and Enlightenment in America: Shaping a New Nation

Have you ever wondered how ideas can change the course of history? In 18th century America, two powerful movements did just that: the Great Awakening and the Enlightenment. These intellectual and spiritual revolutions transformed colonial society, laying the groundwork for American independence and shaping the nation's future.

The Great Awakening and the Enlightenment in America fostered a spirit of religious revival and intellectual inquiry, promoting individualism and questioning traditional authority.

The Great Awakening: A Spiritual Revolution

Imagine a time when religion in the colonies had become routine and uninspiring. Enter the Great Awakening, a religious revival that swept through the American colonies from the 1730s to the 1740s. This movement breathed new life into Christianity, emphasizing personal faith and emotional connections to God.

At the heart of the Great Awakening were charismatic preachers like Jonathan Edwards and George Whitefield. Their fiery sermons drew thousands, preaching that individuals could have a direct relationship with God without relying solely on traditional church authorities. This idea was revolutionary, challenging the established religious order and empowering ordinary people.

The Great Awakening had far-reaching effects beyond religion:

1. It promoted literacy, as more people wanted to read the Bible for themselves.
2. It encouraged questioning authority, a mindset that would later fuel revolutionary ideas.
3. It united colonists across different regions and denominations, fostering a sense of shared American identity.

The Enlightenment: Reason Takes Center Stage

While the Great Awakening stirred souls, the Enlightenment ignited minds. This intellectual movement, which had begun in Europe, emphasized reason, science, and individual rights. In America, Enlightenment ideas found fertile ground, shaping the thinking of colonial leaders and future Founding Fathers.

Key principles of the Enlightenment included:

- The power of human reason to understand the world
- The importance of scientific inquiry and skepticism
- The concept of natural rights and individual liberty
- The idea that governments should serve the people, not the other way around

These ideas challenged traditional sources of authority, including monarchies and established churches. They encouraged people to think critically about their world and their place in it.

The Impact on Colonial America

Together, the Great Awakening and the Enlightenment created a perfect storm of new ideas in colonial America. They fostered a spirit of inquiry, individualism, and resistance to arbitrary authority that would prove crucial in the lead-up to the American Revolution.

Consider how these movements influenced key aspects of American society:

1. Education: Both movements emphasized the importance of learning. This led to the founding of new schools and colleges, including Princeton and Dartmouth.

2. Politics: Enlightenment ideas about natural rights and the social contract directly influenced the Declaration of Independence and the Constitution.

3. Religious Freedom: The Great Awakening's emphasis on personal faith contributed to the principle of religious freedom enshrined in the First Amendment.

4. Social Equality: Both movements challenged traditional hierarchies, promoting the idea that individuals should be judged by their actions and abilities rather than their social status.

A Legacy That Shaped a Nation

The impact of the Great Awakening and the Enlightenment extended far beyond the colonial era. These movements helped shape the American character, fostering values like individualism, religious pluralism, and democratic participation that remain central to American identity today.

As you walk through your school halls or scroll through your social media feed, consider how the legacy of these movements still influences your life. The freedom to express your opinions, practice your faith, or question authority all have roots in this transformative period of American history.

The Great Awakening and the Enlightenment were more than just historical events – they were the intellectual and spiritual sparks that helped ignite the American Revolution and shape the nation that followed. By understanding these movements, we gain insight into the foundations of American society and the ongoing struggle to live up to the ideals of freedom, reason, and individual dignity.

9. The Great Awakening and Enlightenment in America
GUIDED NOTES

I. Key Terms

Define the following terms:

1. Great Awakening: ______________________________

2. Enlightenment: ______________________________

3. Natural rights: ______________________________

II. Main Concept Overview

The Great Awakening and the Enlightenment were two powerful ______________________ that transformed colonial society in the 18th century. The Great Awakening was a ______________________ revival, while the Enlightenment was an ______________________ movement.

III. Matching Section

Match each term with its correct description:

_____ Jonathan Edwards

_____ Enlightenment

_____ Great Awakening

_____ George Whitefield

_____ Declaration of Independence

A. Emphasized reason, science, and individual rights

B. Promoted literacy and questioning authority

C. Charismatic preacher during the Great Awakening

D. Shaped thinking of colonial leaders & future Founding Fathers

E. Directly influenced by Enlightenment ideas

IV. Fill in the Table

Complete the table comparing the Great Awakening and the Enlightenment:

Aspect	Great Awakening	Enlightenment
Primary Focus		
Key Principles		
Impact on Colonial Society		

V. True or False

______ The Great Awakening emphasized personal faith and emotional connections to God.

______ The Enlightenment challenged the power of human reason to understand the world.

______ Both movements fostered a spirit of inquiry and individualism.

______ The Great Awakening had no impact on literacy rates in the colonies.

______ Enlightenment ideas influenced the writing of the Constitution.

VI. Application Question

Describe two ways in which the Great Awakening and the Enlightenment influenced education in colonial America:

____

____

____

VII. Reflection/Summary

In your own words, summarize the main impacts of the Great Awakening and the Enlightenment on colonial America:

____

____

____

How do you think these movements continue to influence American society today? Provide two examples from the article:

____

____

____

9. The Great Awakening and Enlightenment in America - Reflection Questions

1

How might your life be different if the ideas of the Great Awakening and Enlightenment had never spread through colonial America?

Consider how these movements influenced religious practices, education, and individual rights. Think about aspects of your daily life that might be affected, from your educational opportunities to your freedom of expression.

2

How do Enlightenment principles continue to shape political debates in the United States?

Think about current discussions on individual rights, the role of government, and scientific policy. Can you identify arguments that echo Enlightenment ideals?

3

If you were living in colonial America, which movement do you think would have influenced you more - the Great Awakening or the Enlightenment?

Why? Consider your own values and interests. How might these align with the principles of each movement? What aspects of each would you find most compelling?

9. The Great Awakening and Enlightenment in America - Hypotheticals

Scenario 1

What if a group of tech entrepreneurs created an AI-powered "Enlightenment" app?

Consider a situation where a new smartphone app uses artificial intelligence to help users apply reason and critical thinking to their daily decisions and beliefs. The app becomes wildly popular among high school and college students.

a) How might this app affect the way young people approach decision-making and problem-solving?
b) What impact could widespread use of this app have on political engagement among youth?
c) How might educational institutions respond to the popularity of this "Enlightenment" app?

Scenario 2

What if a major social media platform decided to actively promote Enlightenment values?

Imagine that one of the largest social media companies announces a new policy to prioritize content that promotes scientific thinking, reason, and individual rights in users' feeds, similar to Enlightenment ideals.

a) How might this policy change affect the spread of misinformation online?
b) In what ways could this impact political discourse and public opinion on social issues?
c) How might users who disagree with this approach respond to the platform's decision?

9. The Great Awakening and Enlightenment in America - Vocabulary

TERM	DEFINITION
Awakening	
Charismatic	
Enlightenment	
Faith	
Franklin	

9. The Great Awakening and Enlightenment in America - Vocabulary

TERM	DEFINITION
Independence	
Liberty	
Literacy	
Reason	
Revival	

The Great Awakening and Enlightenment in America

L R I F W N H L H S O H W J R L A M Y K A K R E
W F E R U R F Y T D L V C J Q U P L K W W Z V N
Y N Q A K F S V Y E H Y Q P E S X D U J D E O V
K Z F Z S N W R D B A T K D F R A N K L I N M E
M B Z L B O F D O X W N K R T K I G N V R Y V J
W I R P O H N Z N M A K Y A S O P J Q L M C S E
P Y G L O X Y D B I K F I F W R B R N V A F Q N
S M K C W U J N X J E B A W G B D X Y K V V C L
R Y O D Q K D D W D N X X K Y S D U G V J C X I
S A V Q W K D H M V I M J K F R Q J F S Q C G G
W Z Q D T Y B Y V U N U R J N R R S M P Q H G H
R O P G Z I H J N L G Z T K E G J Y T O V Q N T
C E T G J I A X K I H U Z P D S W N Z D U S W E
A S V X E J O L C I N D E P E N D E N C E Y H N
T X F I F T T I J W N X T G O H R B V F X I E M
D P V N V E A T L I B E R T Y Z I S M B N J B E
G I U P F A B E F A M R H K K O P M F I Y A U N
H H Q G X I L R K V O W X X S O S I Z A T Y K T
M W K B Q I J A L K F P Y O J L J L G B I Q C X
O P W S S A R C B F O W Y J L B Z O W X Z T T J
D G T R M Q T Y E O B H H H S I N I R W C F H T
R U L K D A R Y Y Q R Y N K R L E U J Z Q H Y G
J I N N Y N M Z T V N D D D Y L F H Z O T H S Q
O D B F N L P N J C H A R I S M A T I C H V H Y

Revival
Liberty
Faith
Awakening

Reason
Independence
Enlightenment

Literacy
Franklin
Charismatic

The Great Awakening and Enlightenment in America

Across

4. The power of the mind to think, understand, and form judgments logically.

9. Intellectual movement emphasizing reason and individualism.

10. Ability to read and write, promoted by religious revival.

Down

1. Possessing a compelling charm that inspires devotion in others.

2. Religious revival that swept through colonial America.

3. Freedom from control or influence of others.

5. Enlightenment thinker and Founding Father, ______ Benjamin.

6. An improvement in the condition or strength of something, especially religious faith.

7. Strong belief in religious doctrines based on spiritual conviction rather than proof.

8. The state of being free within society from oppressive restrictions.

10. French and Indian War (Seven Years' War)

by 3andB Staff Writer | October 1, 2024

The French and Indian War: A Turning Point in Colonial America

Imagine two giants wrestling for control of a vast, resource-rich land, with smaller groups caught in the middle. This scenario played out in 18th-century North America during the French and Indian War, a conflict that would reshape the continent's future. From 1754 to 1763, this war pitted the British against the French, with Native American tribes aligning on both sides. The outcome would not only determine which European power dominated North America but also set the stage for the American Revolution.

The French and Indian War (1754-1763) was a conflict between Britain and France in North America, driven by territorial disputes, that ultimately led to British dominance in the region and significant colonial discontent.

The Roots of Conflict

At the heart of the French and Indian War lay the struggle for control over the Ohio River Valley, a strategic region rich in fur-trading opportunities and potential for westward expansion. The British colonies, concentrated along the Atlantic coast, were growing rapidly and looking to push inland. Meanwhile, the French had established a vast network of trading posts and alliances with Native American tribes throughout the interior of the continent.

The spark that ignited this powder keg came in 1754 when a young George Washington, then a British colonial officer, led an expedition into the Ohio Valley. His encounter with French forces resulted in a skirmish that would escalate into a full-scale war, eventually drawing in European powers and becoming part of the larger Seven Years' War.

Key Players and Alliances

The conflict wasn't as simple as British versus French. Native American tribes played a crucial role, often tipping the balance of power:

- The British and their colonists: Seeking to expand westward and secure valuable territories.
- The French: Aiming to maintain their control over the fur trade and their colonial empire.
- Iroquois Confederacy: Initially neutral, but eventually siding with the British.
- Many Algonquian-speaking tribes: Allied with the French, with whom they had long-standing trade relationships.

Turning Points of the War

Several key events shaped the course of the conflict:

1. Braddock's Defeat (1755): British General Edward Braddock's disastrous attempt to capture Fort Duquesne (modern-day Pittsburgh) highlighted the challenges of European-style warfare in North America.

2. Conquest of New France (1759-1760): The British capture of Quebec City and Montreal effectively ended French control in Canada.

3. Treaty of Paris (1763): This agreement formally ended the war, with France ceding nearly all its North American territories to Britain.

Impact on Colonial America

The French and Indian War had far-reaching consequences that would shape the future of North America:

1. Shift in Colonial Relationships: The colonies' reliance on British military support during the war paradoxically led to increased desire for autonomy afterward.

2. Financial Strain: The war's enormous cost led Britain to impose new taxes on the colonies, sowing seeds of discontent that would eventually lead to the American Revolution.

3. Westward Expansion: The removal of French power opened up vast territories for British colonial expansion, leading to conflicts with Native American tribes.

4. Military Experience: Colonial militia members, including George Washington, gained valuable military experience that would later be used in the Revolutionary War.

A Continent Transformed

The French and Indian War redrew the map of North America. France lost its North American empire, while Britain gained vast new territories. However, this victory came at a high cost, both financially and in terms of its relationship with the colonies. The war also dramatically altered the balance of power among Native American tribes, many of whom had relied on playing European powers against each other.

Did You Know?

• The war began two years before it was officially declared in Europe, making it one of the first "world wars" in modern history.
• Benjamin Franklin proposed the Albany Plan of Union during this conflict, an early attempt at unifying the colonies that foreshadowed the eventual formation of the United States.

The French and Indian War was more than just a territorial conflict; it was a crucible that forged the future of North America. Its aftermath set in motion events that would lead to the birth of a new nation and forever alter the continent's cultural and political landscape. As we reflect on this pivotal moment in history, we can see how the echoes of this 18th-century conflict still resonate in the world we inhabit today.

10. French and Indian War (Seven Years' War)

GUIDED NOTES

I. Key Terms

1. Ohio River Valley: ____

2. Seven Years' War: ____

3. Treaty of Paris: ____

4. Albany Plan of Union: ____

II. Main Concept Overview

The French and Indian War was a conflict between __________________ and __________________ that lasted from __________ to __________. It was fought primarily over control of the ________________________________, which was valuable for ____________________ and _____________________.

III. Matching Section

Match the term with its correct description:

_____ British colonists	A. Sought to maintain control over the fur trade
_____ French	B. Initially neutral, later sided with the British
_____ Iroquois Confederacy	C. Aimed to expand westward
_____ Algonquian tribes	D. Often allied with the French
_____ George Washington	E. Led an expedition that sparked the war

IV. Fill in the Table

Complete the table with key events of the French and Indian War:

Year	Event	Significance
1754		
1755		
1759-1760		
1763		

V. True or False

______ The French and Indian War had no impact on the American Revolution.

______ The war resulted in France gaining new territories in North America.

______ The conflict was part of a larger global war known as the Seven Years' War.

______ British victory in the war improved their relationship with the colonies.

______ The war provided military experience for future Revolutionary War leaders.

VI. Application Question

Explain how the outcome of the French and Indian War set the stage for the American Revolution. Consider both immediate effects and long-term consequences.

____

____

____

____

VII. Reflection/Summary

Summarize the main impacts of the French and Indian War on Colonial America in your own words. How did this conflict shape the future of North America?

____

____

____

____

____

____

10. French and Indian War (Seven Years' War) - Reflection Questions

1

How might your life be different today if the outcome of the French and Indian War had been reversed, with France emerging victorious?

Consider how this might have affected the development of North America, including language, culture, and political systems. Think about how your community, education, or daily life might be different under French influence rather than British.

2

If you were a colonial leader in 1754, what arguments would you make for or against joining the conflict?

Consider the potential risks and benefits of entering the war. Think about how your decision might affect your colony's relationship with Britain, its economic interests, and its security.

3

In what ways can you draw parallels between the economic factors that led to the French and Indian War and current global conflicts or tensions?

Think about how competition for resources or economic advantages drives international relations today. Consider how economic motivations might be disguised as or intertwined with other justifications for conflict.

10. French and Indian War (Seven Years' War) - Hypotheticals

Scenario 1

Scenario: Suppose that, despite the war's high costs, the British government decides not to impose new taxes on the American colonies, instead finding other means to recover their expenses.

a) How might this decision have affected the relationship between Britain and its American colonies?
b) What impact could this have had on the timeline of the American Revolution?
c) How might this change have influenced the development of colonial governance and economy?

Scenario 2

Scenario: Imagine that 18th-century colonists, soldiers, and Native Americans had access to Twitter, Facebook, and TikTok. News, opinions, and propaganda spread instantly across the colonies and to Europe.

a) How might the rapid spread of information have affected the course of the war?
b) In what ways could social media have influenced alliances between Native American tribes and European powers?
c) How might this scenario compare to the role of social media in modern conflicts?

10. French and Indian War (Seven Years' War) - Vocabulary

TERM	DEFINITION
Alliance	
Expedition	
Frontier	
Militia	
Neutrality	

10. French and Indian War (Seven Years' War) - Vocabulary

TERM	DEFINITION
Skirmish	
Sovereignty	
Territory	
Treaty	
Westward	

The French and Indian War

S Q E M F C K Y F N E U T R A L I T Y D U Y E H

G Z I Q B P R I K N V D E M S N S U W B F V U M

N D U A M J V T A O C G K V P O J Q N D R F L K

F T W P E S V G E A I V H Q N E G Q H R O S S G

K J C K S V Z Z R R L C U H X X Q Q G I N A O Y

E J V W V R V R Q T R L R T J S O B U Q T G L P

K R I M J D B V L Y L I I P C N E P S W I D R L

I E W B U G X X V B Q P T A G P I U K J E Q R M

F H C U O X Z M C N Y M Q O N H O A I L R F B U

T F F L B U D P M B H Y K Y R C R C R K F T H A

J R Z S O V E R E I G N T Y Q Y E X M G N C B X

R S A C P C H W A Y A U R C N X O I I N C X Y X

J M J B A K O D L G K K N R R L Q T S C X X C I

D D D R X N P G I B U Y Y E F J P G H S B O U K

Y Y M A Y W T R E A T Y N D R N N T T R K W G K

C Q O Q A B E O K B R K X G I Y V L X Q J I R Q

R C O P T J L Y C X C T Y W D E M H H S N T U P

U O O A Q Z G D B Q E F F J E M I L I T I A Y F

E X P E D I T I O N D T G F T S H G T R Y G Y Y

E O A D M S V P G Y F R P U K O T B C M D G M U

Y Z U B F W A M S Q Q I Z W E X C W E X A F O L

D P Z L A I F Z X X H J F M O J B E A V H H V C

L S I G P A L V V V O N W T N E G E V R H X X R

U Q Z X M B J I F X U U Z M B V U E P L D F Q U

Westward

Sovereignty

Militia

Alliance

Treaty

Skirmish

Frontier

Territory

Neutrality

Expedition

The French and Indian War

Across

3. The state of not supporting or helping either side in a conflict.

6. Moving or facing toward the west.

9. A journey undertaken for a specific purpose, often exploration.

10. Supreme power or authority over a territory.

Down

1. An area of land under the jurisdiction of a ruler or state.

2. A union between groups, often countries, for a shared purpose.

4. A military force of civilian volunteers, not part of a regular army.

5. A minor fight or brief encounter between small groups of combatants.

7. The border region between explored and unexplored territories.

8. A formal agreement between two or more states.

11. Causes of the American Revolution

by 3andB Staff Writer | October 1, 2024

The Road to Revolution: Understanding the Causes of the American Revolution

Imagine living in a world where your daily life is controlled by a distant power, where your voice in government is limited, and where your hard-earned money is taxed without your consent. This was the reality for many American colonists in the mid-18th century. The American Revolution, a pivotal moment in world history, didn't happen overnight. It was the result of a series of events, policies, and ideologies that gradually pushed the American colonies towards independence. Let's explore the key factors that led to this momentous uprising against British rule.

The American Revolution was largely caused by colonial opposition to British taxation and lack of representation, igniting a desire for independence and self-governance.

The Seeds of Discontent: British Policies and Colonial Reaction

The Aftermath of the French and Indian War

The story of the American Revolution begins in the aftermath of the French and Indian War (1754-1763). While the British emerged victorious, the conflict left them with a mountain of debt. To address this financial burden, the British government turned to its American colonies.

The Sugar Act and Currency Act (1764)

In 1764, the British Parliament passed the Sugar Act, which placed taxes on sugar and other goods. Simultaneously, the Currency Act prohibited colonies from printing their own money. These acts marked the beginning of Britain's attempt to exert greater control over colonial economic affairs.

The Stamp Act Crisis (1765)

The Stamp Act of 1765 proved to be a turning point. This act required colonists to pay a tax on virtually every piece of paper they used, from legal documents to playing cards. For the first time, Parliament was directly taxing the colonists for the purpose of raising revenue, not just regulating trade.

The colonists' response was swift and fierce. The cry of "No taxation without representation" echoed throughout the colonies. This principle, that it was unjust to tax people who had no voice in government, became a rallying cry for the revolutionary cause.

From Resistance to Rebellion

The Townshend Acts and Colonial Boycotts (1767-1770)

Undeterred by colonial resistance, Parliament passed the Townshend Acts in 1767, imposing new taxes on goods such as paint, paper, and tea. In response, colonists organized widespread boycotts of British goods. The tension culminated in the Boston Massacre of 1770, where British soldiers fired on a crowd of protesters, killing five colonists.

The Tea Act and Boston Tea Party (1773)

The Tea Act of 1773, which gave the British East India Company a monopoly on tea sales in the colonies, reignited colonial anger. In a bold act of defiance known as the Boston Tea Party, colonists disguised as Native Americans dumped 342 chests of British tea into Boston Harbor.

The Intolerable Acts (1774)

In retaliation for the Boston Tea Party, Parliament passed a series of punitive laws known as the Intolerable Acts. These laws closed Boston Harbor, restricted town meetings, and gave the British governor greater power. Rather than subduing the colonies, these acts united them in opposition to British rule.

The Ideological Foundations of Revolution

While economic policies and political events were crucial in sparking the revolution, underlying ideological currents played an equally important role:

1. *Enlightenment Ideas:* Colonists were influenced by Enlightenment thinkers like John Locke, who emphasized natural rights and the concept that government power comes from the consent of the governed.

2. *Republican Ideals:* Many colonists embraced republican ideals, believing in a government without a monarch, where power rests with the people.

3. *Colonial Identity:* Years of relative autonomy had fostered a distinct American identity, separate from their British roots.

The Point of No Return

By 1775, the relationship between Britain and its American colonies had reached a breaking point. The battles of Lexington and Concord in April 1775 marked the beginning of armed conflict. In July 1776, the Continental Congress took the final step, issuing the Declaration of Independence.

The American Revolution was not inevitable, but the result of a complex interplay of economic policies, political events, and ideological shifts. Understanding these causes helps us appreciate the birth of the United States not just as a political event, but as a profound transformation in how people viewed their relationship with government and their rights as citizens.

As you reflect on this pivotal moment in history, consider how the principles fought for during the American Revolution continue to shape our world today. How do the ideals of representation, fair taxation, and individual liberty resonate in modern political debates? The echoes of the American Revolution continue to influence not just American society, but democratic movements around the globe.

11. Causes of the American Revolution

GUIDED NOTES

I. Key Terms

1. French and Indian War: ______________________________
2. No taxation without representation: ______________________________
3. Boston Tea Party: ______________________________
4. Intolerable Acts: ______________________________
5. Enlightenment: ______________________________

II. Main Concept Overview

The American Revolution was caused by a series of ____________________, ____________________, and ____________________ factors that gradually pushed the American colonies towards independence from British rule.

III. Match each event with its description:

_____ Sugar Act

_____ Stamp Act

_____ Townshend Acts

_____ Tea Act

_____ Boston Massacre

A. Required tax stamps on paper goods

B. Gave East India Company monopoly on tea sales

C. Taxed sugar and other goods

D. Imposed new taxes on goods like paint and paper

E. British soldiers fired on a crowd, killing five colonists

IV. Fill in the Table: British Acts and Colonial Responses

British Act	Year	Colonial Response
Sugar Act		
Stamp Act		
Townshend Acts		
Tea Act		
Boston Massacre		

V. True or False

______ The French and Indian War left Britain with a significant amount of debt.

______ The Currency Act allowed colonies to print their own money.

______ The Boston Tea Party was a peaceful protest against British tea taxes.

______ The Intolerable Acts united the colonies in opposition to British rule.

______ Enlightenment ideas had no influence on the American Revolution.

VI. Application Question

Explain how the principle of "No taxation without representation" relates to the causes of the American Revolution. Use specific examples from the article to support your answer.

____

____

____

VII. Reflection/Summary

In your own words, summarize the three main factors that led to the American Revolution. How do you think these factors are interconnected?

____

____

____

____

11. Causes of the American Revolution - Reflection Questions

1

How would you react if you were suddenly taxed on everyday items without having a say in the matter?

Think about your daily routine and the items you use regularly. How might unexpected taxes on these items affect your life and your attitude towards the authority imposing them?

2

The principle of "No taxation without representation" was crucial to the American Revolution.

Can you think of any current situations where people might feel they're being subjected to rules or policies without having a say in their creation?

3

Enlightenment ideas played a significant role in shaping revolutionary thought.

What current philosophies or ideologies do you think are influencing political and social movements today? How might they shape future events?

11. Causes of the American Revolution - Hypotheticals

Scenario 1

What if the British Parliament had allowed American representatives?

Imagine that in 1765, instead of imposing the Stamp Act, the British Parliament had invited elected representatives from the American colonies to join them in London.

a) How might this have changed the relationship between Britain and the colonies?
b) What challenges might American representatives have faced in participating in Parliament?
c) Do you think this would have prevented the American Revolution? Why or why not?

Scenario 2

What if the Enlightenment ideas hadn't spread to the colonies?

Imagine that the ideas of Enlightenment thinkers like John Locke had not reached or influenced the American colonies.

a) How might this have affected the colonists' perception of their rights and relationship with Britain?
b) What other ideological foundations might have emerged to challenge British rule?
c) How might the arguments for independence have differed without the influence of Enlightenment thought?

11. Causes of the American Revolution - Vocabulary

TERM	DEFINITION
Revolution	
Parliament	
Taxation	
Representation	
Boycott	

11. Causes of the American Revolution - Vocabulary

TERM	DEFINITION
Autonomy	
Intolerable	
Sovereignty	
Republican	
Independence	

Causes of the American Revolution

K G V X K I I S A R Y H G U C V P F X W Y S S F

D M A N V K T N G B E R N P Y Y E C Z D S X C K

A B S S Z S S L D O J P Z V X G N C Z W A Y X U

H O P A C T Y W H E H X R L J D V E Y V L D L R

L C F G D M D E P I P Y Z E L W J W D X U A J Y

L T B Z E S V C D J M E Z J S P D K Q T C M Z N

J T A U T O N O M Y I P N W U E D S T S F P P C

H K T M X U X H V A N A M D D G N G W G O L Q H

Y D T S X D N R B T T R E R E S Q T Q P R A J A

T T E B O W H Y G X O L G V E N V L A P R S H A

R E P U B L I C A N L I S K P V C V X T V T H P

U Z Y F T L H L Y R E A J A F W Z E U A I Z E I

R G U S O H E V Z H R M N Q U Z L G N V K O E F

E R U V C H E R R B A E Y E A K Z L C I G T N D

V Y V W E A G P F Y B N B T L C B T E S R K W K

O V M H I E N M K U L T H S S I N O V S P Z N V

L Y S M U G I G R Q E R Q Z X Z M H Y M V B X W

U G F F Y Y N W T A X A T I O N X Z L C H L K G

T Q N R M M N F I J M L E E Q V T G W E O T X H

I G Q S O V E R E I G N T Y U B E P P Q T T Q X

O T T Q Y G Q I X H M F A D H L Y K N X P G T Q

N G B F N C Q P T M M U A I Q H X L G Q E F E R

Z L H Y O X H V N J V D O I Z X N Y U D K N X C

J A S H R S O A Q Z D C I W U H C R E W Q Z F N

Independence	Republican	Sovereignty
Intolerable	Autonomy	Boycott
Representation	Taxation	Parliament
Revolution		

Causes of the American Revolution

Across

2. Withdrawing from commercial or social relations as a form of protest.

8. Too extreme to bear, describing certain British acts.

9. The practice of imposing financial charges on individuals or entities by a state.

10. Dramatic change in power or organizational structures, often in a short period.

Down

1. Supreme power or authority, contested between Britain and the colonies.

3. The action of speaking or acting on behalf of someone in a formal capacity.

4. The ultimate goal of the American Revolution, freedom from British control.

5. Relating to a system of government without a monarch.

6. Britain's principal legislative body, responsible for passing the controversial acts.

7. The right or condition of self-government, sought by American colonists.

Turning Points: Key Events of the American Revolution

Picture yourself in 1773 Boston, the air thick with tension. British soldiers patrol the streets, and whispers of rebellion echo through taverns and town squares. This was the backdrop for one of the most pivotal periods in American history: the American Revolution. But what exactly set this monumental struggle in motion, and how did it unfold? Let's explore the key events that shaped the birth of a nation.

The Boston Tea Party: More Than Just a Teatime Protest

On December 16, 1773, the calm waters of Boston Harbor witnessed an unprecedented act of defiance. Colonists, disguised as Native Americans, boarded British ships and dumped 342 chests of tea into the sea. This wasn't just about tea – it was a bold statement against taxation without representation. The Boston Tea Party became the match that lit the revolutionary flame, prompting King George III to impose the harsh Coercive Acts, which the colonists dubbed the "Intolerable Acts."

Key events of the American Revolution include the Boston Tea Party, the Declaration of Independence, and the victory at Yorktown.

The Shot Heard 'Round the World: Lexington and Concord

Fast forward to April 19, 1775. The quiet New England countryside erupted in gunfire as British troops marched towards Concord to seize colonial weapons. The battles of Lexington and Concord marked the official start of the American Revolutionary War. As Ralph Waldo Emerson later wrote, it was here that the "shot heard 'round the world" was fired, signaling the beginning of America's fight for independence.

A Declaration of Independence: From Subjects to Citizens

As the conflict intensified, colonial leaders realized that reconciliation with Britain was no longer possible. On July 4, 1776, the Continental Congress adopted the Declaration of Independence, penned primarily by Thomas Jefferson. This document not only severed ties with Great Britain but also articulated the fundamental principles of human rights and self-governance that would shape the new nation.

Turning the Tide: Saratoga and Valley Forge

The early years of the war were marked by both triumphs and setbacks for the Continental Army. The Battle of Saratoga in 1777 proved to be a crucial turning point. This American victory not only boosted morale but also convinced France to enter the war as an ally, tipping the scales in favor of the revolutionaries.

However, victory didn't come easily. The winter of 1777-1778 saw General Washington's troops endure extreme hardship at Valley Forge. Despite the harsh conditions, this period of training and perseverance transformed the Continental Army into a more disciplined and effective fighting force.

The World Turned Upside Down: Yorktown and Victory

The final act of the revolution played out in Yorktown, Virginia, in 1781. With the help of French naval forces, General Washington's army surrounded British General Cornwallis, forcing his surrender. Legend has it that as the British laid down their arms, their band played "The World Turned Upside Down" – a fitting melody for the birth of a new world order.

Beyond the Battlefield: Shaping a New Nation

The American Revolution wasn't just about military victories; it was a revolution of ideas. The principles of liberty, equality, and self-governance that fueled the revolution would go on to shape the U.S. Constitution and Bill of Rights. These documents established a framework for democratic governance that continues to influence global politics to this day.

Why It Matters: The Revolution's Lasting Impact

You might wonder, "Why should I care about events that happened over 200 years ago?" The American Revolution's impact extends far beyond its time. It inspired revolutions and independence movements worldwide, from France to Latin America. The ideals it championed – such as individual rights and representative government – continue to be central to political debates and struggles for freedom around the globe.

Moreover, understanding the key events of the American Revolution provides crucial context for many of the political and social issues we grapple with today. From debates about the role of government to discussions about civil liberties, the echoes of the revolution resonate in our contemporary world.

As you reflect on these pivotal moments, consider how they've shaped the society you live in today. How do the principles fought for during the American Revolution manifest in your daily life? In what ways are we still working to fulfill the promises of equality and liberty central to the revolutionary cause?

The American Revolution was more than just a series of battles – it was a transformative period that reshaped the political landscape and set the stage for the modern era. By understanding its key events, we gain insight into the foundations of our society and the ongoing struggle to create a more perfect union.

12. Key Events of the American Revolution

GUIDED NOTES

I. Key Terms

1. Boston Tea Party: ____________________
2. Coercive Acts: ____________________
3. Continental Congress: ____________________
4. Declaration of Independence: ____________________
5. Valley Forge: ____________________

II. Main Concept Overview

The American Revolution was a period of ____________________ and ____________________ that led to the birth of the United States. It began with acts of defiance against British rule and ended with the creation of a new ____________________ based on principles of ____________________ and ____________________.

III. Matching Section

Match each event with its significance:

_____ Boston Tea Party

_____ Lexington and Concord

_____ Declaration of Independence

_____ Battle of Saratoga

_____ Battle of Yorktown

A. Official start of the American Revolutionary War

B. Crucial American victory that secured French alliance

C. Protest against taxation without representation

D. Document that severed ties with Great Britain

E. Final major battle leading to British surrender

IV. Fill in the Table

Complete the table with information from the article:

Event	Date	Significance
Boston Tea Party		
Battles of Lexington and Concord		
Adoption of Declaration of Independence		
Winter at Valley Forge		
Battle of Yorktown		

V. True or False

_____ The Boston Tea Party was primarily about the colonists' love for coffee.

_____ The Battle of Saratoga was a turning point that convinced France to ally with the Americans.

_____ Valley Forge was a period of easy living for the Continental Army.

_____ The Declaration of Independence was written primarily by George Washington.

_____ The American Revolution inspired other independence movements around the world.

VI. Application Question

Describe how the principles fought for during the American Revolution (such as individual rights and representative government) are reflected in modern society. Provide at least two specific examples.

____

____

____

____

VII. Reflection/Summary

In your own words, summarize the main events of the American Revolution and explain why they were significant. How do you think these events have shaped the United States as we know it today?

____

____

____

____

12. Key Events of the American Revolution - Reflection Questions

1

How might your life be different if the American Revolution had never occurred?

Consider the principles of democracy and individual rights that emerged from the Revolution. How do these shape your daily life and future opportunities?

2

How does the Declaration of Independence continue to influence global politics today?

Reflect on the document's key principles. Can you identify any current events or international situations where these ideas are being championed or challenged?

3

In what ways is the American experiment in self-governance still evolving?

Consider current debates about voting rights, representation, and the role of government. How do these connect to the ideals of the American Revolution, and what do you think the next steps should be in fulfilling the promise of democracy?

12. Key Events of the American Revolution - Hypotheticals

Scenario 1

Scenario: What if George Washington had accepted the offer to become king? Imagine that after the war, when some suggested making Washington king, he had accepted the offer instead of retiring to Mount Vernon.

a) How would this decision have altered the structure of the new American government?
b) What implications would this have had for the principles of the revolution, such as rejecting monarchy and promoting democracy?
c) How might this have affected Washington's legacy and the office of the presidency?

Scenario 2

Scenario: Student Body President Goes Rogue

After a heated student election, the winning candidate for student body president starts making unilateral decisions without consulting the student council, similar to how some wanted George Washington to become a king.

a) How might this affect the structure and effectiveness of student government?
b) What actions could other student leaders or the school administration take in response?
c) How does this scenario reflect the importance of checks and balances in government?

12. Key Events of the American Revolution - Vocabulary

TERM	DEFINITION
Revolution	
Rebellion	
Taxation	
Independence	
Allies	

12. Key Events of the American Revolution - Vocabulary

TERM	DEFINITION
Constitution	
Liberty	
Sovereignty	
Patriot	
Loyalist	

Key Events of the American Revolution

Q U K O B O L I U I X U V V R E B E L L I O N A

L R Q L U Q V G T S E X E H H X T P A M K Y D H

D I N R Y J N O C D U W M Z O K Y H F X Z E F X

R B B C L X Q L F Z T Q I H P A T R I O T P N W

Z E D E L U S H K E S Y H M B H U I K O T W T W

F B V R R T P B C H I J X M G T C N G N F K C K

Y T H O B T X T I L T K H M R B Q D Q F D I N M

E M R Z L S Y K J G I A F K Y O R E N X C J R O

I Q S I R U H F U U Q U X N Q D X P G U E S V X

B T N D E V T Q Q N M A A A O Q L E X O P V C Q

W V Y C Z O Q I O N O G P V T U J N M S L N Q N

N D Y V F B P R O I F V U D D I U D L S R V Q C

A W T Y S R F K X N N J Q X K Y O E W R S A U D

N G S K N R L H D F S N B A B R W N X L E N J O

Y I O H V V D Z U P V S H D C M M C M D B C P B

T Y V I Q P H P B V D J H B O K Q E M X W I O W

O F E I E T X W L Y C O N S T I T U T I O N F Y

R B R H D S J V Y B M N R Q O Z O N W C L C T O

D K E M N R P P K C P D Q V V F U A G M U S G Q

X Z I E U E C H M E A L L I E S H M M Y B H Y E

Z W G Z C Y B Z X U U N O P Q G S W C G R H V N

K I N X U O F Y M T M N C Q R W V T R M U K K K

X Q T Z P G L N W N R G L O Q W L O Y A L I S T

F R Y G Y D L T P G H H C A M I X F I T A D I Z

Loyalist

Patriot

Sovereignty

Liberty

Constitution

Allies

Independence

Taxation

Rebellion

Revolution

Key Events of the American Revolution

Across

6. An act of armed resistance to an established government or leader.

7. The practice of a government collecting money from its citizens to pay for public services.

9. A body of fundamental principles or established precedents according to which a state or organization is governed.

10. A person who remains loyal to the established ruler or government, especially in the face of a revolt.

Down

1. A person who vigorously supports their country and is prepared to defend it against enemies or detractors.

2. Dramatic change in power or organizational structures.

3. Freedom from outside control; not depending on another's authority.

4. Supreme power or authority.

5. States or groups formally cooperating for a military or other purpose.

8. The state of being free within society from oppressive restrictions imposed by authority on one's way of life, behavior, or political views.

13. The Declaration of Independence

by 3andB Staff Writer | October 1, 2024

The Declaration of Independence: America's Founding Document

There is a crowded square in 1776, the air thick with tension and excitement. A voice rings out, reading words that would change the course of history: "We hold these truths to be self-evident, that all men are created equal..." These powerful words marked the birth of a new nation and the beginning of a grand experiment in democracy. But what led to this momentous declaration, and why does it continue to resonate with us today?

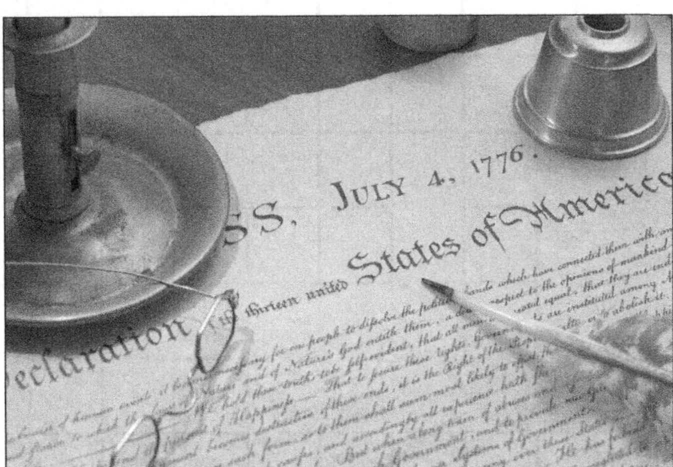

The Declaration of Independence, adopted on July 4, 1776, proclaimed the American colonies' separation from British rule and articulated the principles of individual liberty and government by consent.

The Declaration of Independence, adopted by the Continental Congress on July 4, 1776, was more than just a formal announcement of the American colonies' separation from Great Britain. It was a bold statement of human rights and a blueprint for a new form of government. In this article, we'll explore the origins, content, and lasting impact of this revolutionary document.

The Road to Independence

By 1776, tensions between the American colonies and Great Britain had reached a boiling point. Years of unfair taxation, lack of representation in Parliament, and increasingly oppressive British policies had pushed the colonists to the brink of rebellion. The battles of Lexington and Concord in 1775 had already ignited the American Revolution, but many colonists still hoped for reconciliation with the mother country.

However, as the conflict escalated, it became clear that a formal break was necessary. In June 1776, the Continental Congress appointed a committee to draft a declaration of independence. Thomas Jefferson, a young Virginia lawyer and plantation owner, was chosen as the primary author, with input from John Adams, Benjamin Franklin, and others.

The Structure and Content of the Declaration

The Declaration of Independence is divided into four main sections:

1. Introduction: This section explains the purpose of the document and introduces the idea of "natural rights."

2. Preamble: Perhaps the most famous part, beginning with "We hold these truths to be self-evident," it outlines the philosophical justification for independence.

3. List of Grievances: This section details the colonists' complaints against King George III, providing evidence of his "repeated injuries and usurpations."

4. Conclusion: The final part formally declares the colonies' independence and pledges the signers' lives, fortunes, and sacred honor to the cause.

The document's most revolutionary aspect was its assertion of individual rights and the idea that government derives its power from the consent of the governed. These concepts, influenced by Enlightenment thinkers like John Locke, would form the foundation of American democracy.

The Declaration's Impact and Legacy

The immediate effect of the Declaration was to unite the colonies in their fight for independence. It galvanized support for the revolutionary cause and helped secure crucial foreign alliances, particularly with France.

But the Declaration's influence extends far beyond the American Revolution. Its principles have inspired freedom movements around the world, from the French Revolution to the civil rights movement in the United States. The document's assertion of equality and inalienable rights continues to challenge us to live up to these ideals.

It's important to note, however, that the Declaration's promise of equality was not initially extended to all. Women, enslaved people, and Native Americans were excluded from its protections. The struggle to fully realize the Declaration's principles has been a central theme in American history.

The Declaration in Your Life

You might wonder how a document written nearly 250 years ago relates to your life today. Consider this: every time you vote, express your opinion freely, or participate in your school's student government, you're exercising rights that trace back to the ideals expressed in the Declaration of Independence.

Moreover, understanding the Declaration can help you critically analyze current events. When you hear debates about government policies or civil rights issues, you can refer back to the principles outlined in this founding document. It provides a framework for considering questions of liberty, equality, and the role of government in our lives.

The Declaration of Independence stands as a testament to the power of ideas to shape history. Its bold assertion of human rights and self-government set a new standard for political thought and action. As you continue your studies of American history, keep in mind the profound impact of this document and consider how its principles continue to shape our nation and the world.

Did You Know?

- The original Declaration of Independence is housed in the National Archives in Washington, D.C., where it's protected by bulletproof glass and monitored for any signs of deterioration.
- John Hancock's famous large signature was likely so big because, as president of the Continental Congress, he signed first on a large, blank space.

13. The Declaration of Independence

GUIDED NOTES

I. Key Terms

Define the following terms based on the article:

1. Declaration of Independence: ___________________________________

2. Continental Congress: ___________________________________

3. Natural rights: ___________________________________

II. Main Concept Overview

The Declaration of Independence was a ____________________ proclamation of ____________________ and ____________________. It was adopted by the Continental Congress on ____________________, ____________________.

III. Matching

Match each term with its correct description:

_____ Thomas Jefferson A. Helped unite the colonies in their fight

_____ John Locke B. Primary author of the Declaration

_____ King George III C. Enlightenment thinker who influenced the Declaration

_____ The Declaration D. Subject of the colonists' complaints

IV. Fill in the Table

Complete the table with information from the article:

Section of the Declaration	Purpose
Introduction	
Preamble	
List of Grievances	
Conclusion	

V. True or False

______ The Declaration of Independence immediately granted equal rights to all people in America.

______ The document helped secure foreign alliances for the colonies.

______ The Declaration of Independence has only influenced American history.

______ The principles of the Declaration continue to be debated and applied today.

______ The original Declaration is on display in Philadelphia.

VI. Application Question

How does the Declaration of Independence relate to your life today? Provide two specific examples from the article.

____

____

____

VII. Reflection/Summary

In your own words, summarize the main points of the article and explain why the Declaration of Independence is considered a founding document of the United States.

____

____

____

____

____

____

13. The Declaration of Independence - Reflection Questions

1

How might your life be different if the Declaration of Independence had never been written?

Consider the rights and freedoms you enjoy today. Think about how the principles outlined in the Declaration have shaped American society and government. How might your daily life, education, or future opportunities be affected if these ideas had never been articulated or fought for?

2

If you were to write a "personal declaration of independence," what rights or principles would you include, and why?

Think about the values and freedoms that are most important to you. Consider both personal liberties and responsibilities to others. How would your declaration reflect your beliefs about individual rights and the role of community or government in your life?

3

How do you see the tension between individual rights and collective responsibility playing out in current events or issues in your community?

Consider recent news stories or local debates. How do they reflect the ongoing challenge of balancing personal freedoms with societal needs? Think about how the principles of the Declaration might inform these discussions.

Scenario 1

Scenario: Digital Rights Declaration
In 2030, as artificial intelligence and data collection become increasingly pervasive, a coalition of tech experts and civil rights activists drafts a "Declaration of Digital Independence." This document, inspired by the original Declaration of Independence, asserts the inalienable digital rights of individuals in the face of corporate and governmental control of personal data.

a) What "self-evident truths" or rights might this Digital Declaration include?
b) How might the structure and language of the original Declaration of Independence be adapted for this modern context?
c) What challenges might the authors of this declaration face, and how do these compare to the challenges faced by the original Declaration's signers?

Scenario 2

Scenario: Alternative History
Imagine an alternate 1776 where the Continental Congress decides not to issue the Declaration of Independence, instead choosing to continue negotiating with Britain for greater autonomy within the empire.

a) How might this decision have affected the course of the American Revolution?
b) What potential long-term effects could this have had on the development of democracy and individual rights in North America?
c) How might world history have been different if the United States had not become an independent nation at that time?

13. The Declaration of Independence - Vocabulary

TERM	DEFINITION
Independence	
Revolution	
Declaration	
Continental Congress	
Grievances	

TERM	DEFINITION
Inalienable	
Oppressive	
Reconciliation	
Usurpations	
Preamble	

13: WORD SEARCH

The Declaration of Independence

C H B Z F Y X D O R D Z M B P W B Q R X P G E K

R E V O L U T I O N K P X K X N A Y M P E K H V

D A K R M I N A L I E N A B L E T M R B I B E Q

I G R I E V A N C E S I R R I K Y F O H U T M U

H K O U W G M X W D T R T U D I Z B U W W E B S

G L O B P J F I U R L X N C O B N U A Z N Y P P

E J T K S R B D U Y U U E Y J P L U N X C T O P

X R T X V W E J R J T I S V R J P Y Y H G R B Y

L M Z M J V F A D P N Q Z E E W D R U B T S B C

L I G A G R Z L M D Y G G V C J R P E Z D K L Q

U N K T N R M W E B C K Y P O M S T W S I M B A

S D J W R Z O D R D L B D T N N D R Z Z S R U W

U E T D Z E J U L I H E T Z C Y L H E P J I J E

R P Y N E N X A S C W W V R I F D A Z C S D V C

P E N L S C I X O V X E W J L K B F F V T S E E

A N T S L L L I O D F O T U I O B I W E R I Q N

T D U I H B M A I O N Q N U A R Z C P S Q F G U

I E D Y H W J S R R K V I F T K T V I O R R K C

O N B Q H F B T X A R X V P I S N X Y Y T R M E

N C E G G Z V R S O T X M A O C V A Q D T D B P

S E L M G R X P F H I I W N N X M P E K S U K R

C O N T I N E N T A L C O N G R E S S Z Y R S O

W Q V N P U Y M H Y B B N N R W S Y D P Z I V A

C Q F K K A V Q U U P D K N U Z P K L H L M G U

Preamble

Usurpations

Reconciliation

Oppressive

Inalienable

Grievances

Continental Congress

Declaration

Revolution

Independence

The Declaration of Independence

Across

7. A preliminary or preparatory statement; an introduction.

8. Unable to be taken away from or given away by the possessor.

9. The restoration of friendly relations.

10. The action of taking a position of power or importance illegally or by force.

Down

1. The governing body of the American colonies during the Revolutionary War.

2. Freedom from control or influence of another or others.

3. Real or supposed grounds for complaint, especially against authority.

4. A fundamental change in political organization; overthrow of a government.

5. Unjustly inflicting hardship and constraint, especially on a minority or other subordinate group.

6. A formal or explicit statement or announcement.

14. The Articles of Confederation

by 3andB Staff Writer | October 1, 2024

The Articles of Confederation: America's First Constitution

A newly formed country, fresh from revolution, is trying to govern itself for the first time. This was the challenge facing the United States after declaring independence from Great Britain in 1776. The solution? The Articles of Confederation, America's first attempt at creating a national government. This document laid the groundwork for how the thirteen original states would operate as a unified nation, shaping the early years of American independence and setting the stage for the eventual creation of the U.S. Constitution.

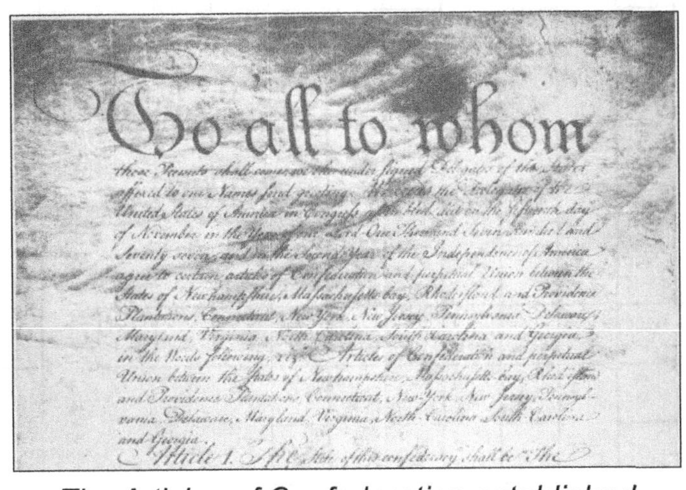

The Articles of Confederation established the first governing framework for the United States, creating a weak central government that struggled to manage the country's needs.

The Birth of a New Government

The Articles of Confederation were drafted in 1777, during the heat of the American Revolutionary War. As the colonies fought for independence, they also grappled with how to govern themselves once that independence was won. The Articles represented a delicate balance between the desire for a united front against Britain and the states' reluctance to give up their individual powers.

Key features of the Articles included:

1. A loose confederation of sovereign states
2. A unicameral (one-chamber) Congress as the central governing body
3. Equal representation for each state in Congress, regardless of population
4. The requirement of unanimous consent to amend the Articles

The drafting process was led by John Dickinson, and the final document was adopted by the Continental Congress in 1777. However, it wasn't until 1781 that the Articles were fully ratified by all thirteen states, with Maryland being the last to approve.

Strengths and Weaknesses

The Articles of Confederation had both strengths and weaknesses. On the positive side, they:

• Successfully guided the country through the remainder of the Revolutionary War
• Established a framework for westward expansion through the Northwest Ordinance of 1787
• Allowed states to retain significant autonomy, preventing a potentially tyrannical central government
• Created a system for admitting new states to the Union on equal footing with existing states

However, the weaknesses of the Articles became increasingly apparent over time:

• The central government lacked the power to levy taxes, relying instead on voluntary contributions from states
• There was no executive branch to enforce laws or judicial branch to interpret them

• Foreign policy was difficult to conduct effectively, as the government couldn't enforce treaties
• Economic issues arose due to the lack of a common currency and the inability to regulate interstate commerce
• The requirement of a 9/13 majority to pass laws often led to governmental paralysis

Real-World Impact

The shortcomings of the Articles of Confederation had real-world consequences. For example, Shays' Rebellion in 1786-1787 highlighted the central government's inability to respond effectively to domestic crises. When Massachusetts farmers, led by Daniel Shays, rebelled against high taxes and farm foreclosures, the federal government couldn't raise an army to suppress the uprising. This event underscored the need for a stronger central authority.

Another significant issue was the government's inability to repay war debts. Without the power to tax, the Confederation Congress struggled to meet its financial obligations to soldiers and foreign creditors, damaging the young nation's credit and reputation.

The Path to the Constitution

As the limitations of the Articles became clear, leaders like James Madison, Alexander Hamilton, and George Washington advocated for reform. In 1787, delegates gathered in Philadelphia for what became known as the Constitutional Convention. Originally intending to revise the Articles, they instead drafted an entirely new document: the U.S. Constitution.

The Constitution addressed many of the weaknesses of the Articles by:

• Creating a stronger federal government with executive, legislative, and judicial branches
• Granting the central government the power to levy taxes and regulate interstate commerce
• Establishing a system of checks and balances to prevent any one branch from becoming too powerful
• Implementing a bicameral legislature with representation based on both population and state equality

The shift from the Articles to the Constitution wasn't without controversy. Debates raged between Federalists, who supported a strong central government, and Anti-Federalists, who feared the loss of state sovereignty. The compromise was the addition of the Bill of Rights, which protected individual liberties and state powers.

The Articles of Confederation, while flawed, were a crucial stepping stone in America's journey toward effective self-governance. They represented the young nation's first attempt at balancing state sovereignty with the need for national unity. The lessons learned from the Articles' strengths and weaknesses directly informed the creation of the U.S. Constitution, shaping the federal system we know today. Understanding the Articles of Confederation provides valuable insights into the evolution of American democracy and the ongoing balance between state and federal powers.

Did You Know?

• John Hanson, elected in 1781, was technically the first "President of the United States in Congress Assembled" under the Articles of Confederation, predating George Washington's presidency under the Constitution.
• The Articles of Confederation were officially in effect for only eight years, from 1781 to 1789, when they were replaced by the U.S. Constitution.

14. The Articles of Confederation

GUIDED NOTES

I. Key Terms

1. Articles of Confederation: ______________________________

2. Unicameral: ______________________________

3. Northwest Ordinance: ______________________________

4. Shays' Rebellion: ______________________________

5. Constitutional Convention: ______________________________

II. Main Concept Overview

The Articles of Confederation were America's first attempt at creating a ____________________ government following the ____________________ War. They established a loose confederation of ____________________ states with a ____________________ Congress as the central governing body. The Articles were drafted in __________ and fully ratified in __________.

III. Matching Section

Match the term with its correct description:

_____ Articles of Confederation	A. Highlighted the central government's inability to respond to crises
_____ Northwest Ordinance	B. America's first constitution
_____ Shays' Rebellion	C. Established a framework for westward expansion
_____ James Madison	D. Replaced the Articles of Confederation
_____ U.S. Constitution	E. Advocated for reform of the Articles

IV. True/False

_____ The Articles of Confederation created a strong central government.

_____ Under the Articles, each state had equal representation in Congress.

_____ The central government could levy taxes under the Articles.

_____ Foreign policy was difficult to conduct effectively under the Articles.

_____ The Articles of Confederation were in effect from 1781 to 1789.

V. Fill in the Table

Complete the table comparing features under the Articles of Confederation and the U.S. Constitution:

Feature	Articles of Confederation	U.S. Constitution
Central government power		
Branches of government		
Ability to levy taxes		
State representation		
Amendment process		

VI. Application Question

Describe how the Articles of Confederation impacted the government's ability to handle economic issues, and explain how this was addressed in the U.S. Constitution.

VII. Reflection/Summary

Summarize two strengths and two weaknesses of the Articles of Confederation mentioned in the article. How did these factors contribute to the creation of the U.S. Constitution?

14. The Articles of Confederation - Reflection Questions

1

How might your daily life be different if the United States was still governed by the Articles of Confederation instead of the Constitution?

Consider how the weak central government under the Articles might affect national policies, economic stability, and individual rights. Think about aspects like currency, interstate travel, and national security.

2

If you were a citizen during the time of the Articles of Confederation, would you have supported changing to the Constitution?

Why or why not? Reflect on the benefits and drawbacks of both systems. Consider factors such as state sovereignty, individual liberties, and the need for a strong national government.

3

How did the experience with the Articles of Confederation shape the principles of the U.S. Constitution?

What lessons do you think the Founding Fathers learned? Think about the specific weaknesses of the Articles and how they were addressed in the Constitution. Consider the balance between state and federal powers.

Scenario 1

Scenario 1: Economic Crisis
Imagine it's 1788, and the United States is still governed by the Articles of Confederation. A severe economic depression hits, with widespread unemployment and a collapse in interstate trade. Several states begin printing their own currency to stimulate local economies, while others impose tariffs on goods from neighboring states.

a) How might the central government under the Articles of Confederation respond to this crisis?
b) What potential consequences could arise from states taking individual actions to address the economic issues?
c) How might this scenario have influenced the debate over the need for a stronger central government?

Scenario 2

Scenario 3: Westward Expansion Dispute
The year is 1792, and the Articles of Confederation remain the law of the land. As settlers move westward, a dispute arises between Pennsylvania and Virginia over newly settled territories. Both states claim ownership of the same land and have sent militias to enforce their claims.

a) How would the government under the Articles of Confederation be equipped to handle this interstate dispute?
b) What potential consequences could arise from states using their militias in this way?
c) How might this scenario influence discussions about the need for a federal judiciary system?

14. The Articles of Confederation - Vocabulary

TERM	DEFINITION
Articles	
Confederation	
Congress	
Federalists	
Ordinance	

TERM	DEFINITION
Ratification	
Rebellion	
Unanimous	
Unicameral	
Levy	

14: WORD SEARCH

The Articles of Confederation

```
D O Q G Y B O L W Q R L X S V Q F V O H F X K W
C H T H Z P J T Z C O Z M X N A A L B H N O Q B
I V Z X F R J V H Y P W S O R D I N A N C E N N
R A T I F I C A T I O N H M Z O W J I M X F A Z
P A I M M F F C J Z Q M R C T P I T W J U R W Z
Q R M S L S X Z C J H G S F L G B O K W T A Y X
U T M A L U M O E M E W E P K R H M O H B E W H
T I T O Z J V K K M K Q Z X R E C O T S V E Y S
Z C E M C X T K U B V G S E O B Z U M L R C J K
F L M V M X A D T N L G X O G E X Z O C X O G J
E E G A F R D T N E I M I R C L V D Z O I R Q A
D S D D H K J M E X W C H G O L C M I O G X D Z
E V V H U B P J V U Y N A Y N I A O Z Y Q R U S
R F G L H K L J D D U H M M F O G F N C W C E U
A F U N A N I M O U S U X B E N W K B G E C E T
L Z H P T C A U A I D V M M D R C Z A U R G E X
I M L O Z G V T Z A L W X H E R A H P O X E L K
S P V N E O F C A B J I Z K R U V L O P T I S X
T K A E I L W O B R V I U L A R Q W Q D F E P S
S J X Z C H N P V E Z Z J E T H T J L F R N C T
Z Q Y R A X D Q J J O G E V I F B O D O X S Y G
G R A L D Y P T R X T I F Y O V Q P G V A O Y X
H Q Z N N W D I M B F N M H N A I O L O O S N E
U D T Q V W D V Y Y T M P R Z A C V C E N T I R
```

Levy

Unicameral

Unanimous

Rebellion

Ratification

Ordinance

Federalists

Congress

Confederation

Articles

The Articles of Confederation

Across

2. Having or consisting of a single legislative chamber.

4. A law or regulation, like the one establishing rules for western territories.

6. The process of approving and giving formal consent to a constitution.

7. Supporters of a strong central government during the Constitutional debates.

10. America's first attempt at a national governing document.

Down

1. Agreed by all parties, required for amending the Articles.

3. A union of sovereign states bound together by a central government.

5. The unicameral governing body under this early American system.

8. An armed uprising against authority, like the one led by Daniel Shays.

9. To impose or collect, something the early government couldn't do with taxes.

15. The Constitution and the Bill of Rights

by 3andB Staff Writer | October 1, 2024

The Constitution and the Bill of Rights: Foundations of American Democracy

The nation is without a rulebook, laws can change on a whim and citizens' rights are uncertain. This was the challenge facing the newly independent United States in the late 18th century. The solution? The Constitution and the Bill of Rights—two documents that would shape the course of American history and inspire democratic movements worldwide. These foundational texts established the framework for the U.S. government and protected individual liberties, creating a blueprint for democracy that continues to guide the nation today.

The Birth of the Constitution: A Need for Change

After gaining independence from Britain, the United States operated under the Articles of Confederation. This system proved weak and ineffective, leading to economic struggles and interstate conflicts. The central government lacked the power to levy taxes, regulate commerce, or enforce laws. Recognizing the need for a stronger central government, delegates from the states gathered in Philadelphia in 1787 for the Constitutional Convention.

Crafting a New Government

The delegates faced a monumental task: creating a government strong enough to unite the nation, yet limited enough to prevent tyranny. Through months of debate and compromise, they developed a system of checks and balances and separation of powers. The Constitution established three branches of government:

1. ***Legislative*** (Congress): Makes laws
2. ***Executive*** (President): Enforces laws
3. ***Judicial*** (Supreme Court): Interprets laws

This structure ensured that no single branch could become too powerful, safeguarding against the tyranny the colonists had fought to escape.

Key Principles of the Constitution

The Constitution is built on several fundamental principles:

- *Federalism:* Divides power between national and state governments
- *Popular Sovereignty:* The people are the source of government authority
- *Limited Government:* The government's powers are defined and restricted
- Separation of Powers: Divides power among the three branches
- Checks and Balances: Each branch can limit the powers of the others

The Constitution and Bill of Rights establish the framework for the U.S. government and protect individual freedoms and rights.

These principles work together to create a stable yet flexible system of government, capable of adapting to changing times while preserving core democratic values.

The Bill of Rights: Protecting Individual Liberties - A Crucial Addition

While the Constitution established the government's structure, many feared it didn't adequately protect individual rights. To address these concerns, the first ten amendments to the Constitution—known as the Bill of Rights—were ratified in 1791.

Fundamental Freedoms

The Bill of Rights guarantees essential liberties, including:

- Freedom of speech, religion, press, assembly, and petition (1st Amendment)
- Right to bear arms (2nd Amendment)
- Protection against unreasonable searches and seizures (4th Amendment)
- Right to due process and protection against self-incrimination (5th Amendment)
- Right to a speedy and public trial by an impartial jury (6th Amendment)
- Protection against cruel and unusual punishment (8th Amendment)

These rights form the cornerstone of American civil liberties, protecting citizens from government overreach and ensuring individual freedoms.

Relevance Today

The Constitution and Bill of Rights continue to shape American life in countless ways. From Supreme Court decisions on free speech to debates over gun control, these documents remain at the heart of legal and political discussions. They provide a framework for addressing new challenges, such as privacy rights in the digital age or the balance between national security and individual liberties.

As a high school student, you encounter the impact of these documents daily. Your right to express opinions, practice your religion, or petition for change in your school all stem from the protections enshrined in the Constitution and Bill of Rights. Understanding these foundational texts empowers you to participate fully in American democracy and to appreciate the rights and responsibilities of citizenship.

The Constitution and the Bill of Rights are more than historical documents—they are living texts that continue to guide and shape American democracy. By establishing a system of government and protecting individual liberties, they created a foundation for a nation that could grow, adapt, and strive towards the ideals of freedom and justice. As you study these documents, remember that you are part of this ongoing story, with the power and responsibility to uphold and shape the principles they represent.

Did You Know?

The Constitution has been amended 27 times since its ratification, with the most recent amendment ratified in 1992. This ongoing process of amendment demonstrates the document's ability to evolve with the nation it governs.

15. The Constitution and the Bill of Rights

GUIDED NOTES

I. Key Terms

1. Constitution: ______________________________

2. Bill of Rights: ______________________________

3. Federalism: ______________________________

4. Checks and Balances: ______________________________

II. The Need for the Constitution

1. After independence, the United States initially operated under the ______________________.

2. This system proved weak because it lacked the power to:

   a. ______________________ b. ______________________

   c. ______________________

3. To address these issues, delegates gathered in ____________ in the year ______ for the Constitutional Convention.

III. Structure of the Government

Fill in the table with the three branches of government and their primary functions:

Branch	Primary Function
1.	
2.	
3.	

IV. Principles of the Constitution

Match each principle with its correct description:

_____ Popular Sovereignty	A. Divides power between national and state governments
_____ Limited Government	B. Each branch can limit the powers of the others
_____ Federalism	C. The people are the source of government authority
_____ Separation of Powers	D. The government's powers are defined and restricted
_____ Checks and Balances	E. Divides power among the three branches

V. The Bill of Rights

1. The Bill of Rights consists of the first ______ amendments to the Constitution.
2. It was ratified in the year ____________.
3. List three fundamental freedoms guaranteed by the Bill of Rights:
   a. ____
   b. ____
   c. ____

VI. True or False

_____ The Constitution cannot be changed or amended.

_____ The Bill of Rights protects citizens from government overreach.

_____ The three branches of government are entirely independent with no oversight of each other.

_____ As a student, the Constitution and Bill of Rights have no impact on your daily life.

_____ The Constitution established a system of checks and balances to prevent tyranny.

VII. Short Answer

1. Explain why the Articles of Confederation were considered ineffective:

____

____

2. How does the Constitution remain relevant in addressing modern challenges? Provide an example:

____

____

15. The Constitution and the Bill of Rights - Reflection Questions

1

How might your daily life be different if the Bill of Rights didn't exist?

Consider specific freedoms you enjoy and how their absence would impact you. Your ability to express opinions, practice religion, or feel secure in your personal belongings. How would the absence of these protections change your behavior or choices?

2

The Constitution has been amended 27 times since its ratification. If you could propose a new amendment, what would it be and why?

What current issues or rights do you think need constitutional protection? How would your amendment improve American democracy or address modern challenges?

3

How does the system of checks and balances affect the way decisions are made in the United States?

Can you think of a recent event or issue where this system played a visible role? News stories about conflicts between branches of government. How did the system of checks and balances come into play? What might have happened without this system?

Scenario 1

Scenario: Social Media and Free Speech

The federal government passes a law requiring all social media platforms to remove posts containing “misleading information” within 24 hours or face hefty fines. A group of citizens argues this violates their First Amendment rights.

a) How might this law conflict with the First Amendment’s protection of free speech?
b) What challenges might arise in defining “misleading information”?
c) How could this scenario demonstrate the system of checks and balances in action?

Scenario 2

Scenario: Technology and Privacy Rights

A new type of security scanner is developed that can detect hidden weapons from a distance, but it also reveals other personal items and medical devices under clothing. The government wants to implement these scanners in all public spaces for safety reasons.

a) What key points from the article would you emphasize in your videos?
b) How would you connect historical events to issues that teenagers care about today?
c) What creative approaches could you use to make US history more appealing to a young audience?

15. The Constitution and the Bill of Rights - Vocabulary

TERM	DEFINITION
Constitution	
Bill of Rights	
Federalism	
Checks and Balances	
Separation of Powers	

TERM	DEFINITION
Popular Sovereignty	
Limited Government	
Amendment	
Liberty	
Due Process	

The Constitution and the Bill of Rights

G M I J R Z I E B L A P D P I H G F U B Q A H W
D L M J B M Z S A U J A G J T W S K H C P A S V
L K O L T J R A L J Q B Y U R Y Q Q T H A O E E
H W Y I H F M W Z A S G X W W P Z M V C R V P X
C P C B C B X C K V L O S F X L O I G P Z T A Q
Z X V E C T O X J W Y M K Z I G O S P Q O N R H
C R F R P O P U L A R S O V E R E I G N T Y A F
J C O T O L N G Q T F G N U O H Z R E H K G T U
G H B Y W Q P S Q K F V X X G G V Y T X L H I T
K E I K Z O S H T S R E U W A X O K Y K G Y O N
Z C L J K S V I U I X J D A G X F C W X C X N U
M K L A P A L E P E T Y M E W J L K D G H J O I
G S O Y P Y Q L F O V U H H R O H D I L A O F Z
X A F O R S E R F E G Y T M F A H X V B U L P D
N N R R H T D W T W T X I I N N L Y P H O J O U
A D I X W G X X V O V G O G O D U I V D K U W E
M B G O I A I W N O N V P A V N G I S B V X E P
E A H P Z N B B R J P P P R Q Z R E T M G I R R
N L T P E J H F R Y V Q G R H I J F W L C J S O
D A S A Y D L I M I T E D G O V E R N M E N T C
M N B I K Q K F V Z V U O X D Q I O O C D A P E
E C S F H I F P H E D U I K U L P S X U F H F S
N E G M C L X F D D F R Y L T C F C Y T R D L S
T S P J D T J V S Y T Z W L I J B M D H W A V T

Due Process
Liberty
Amendment
Limited Government
Popular Sovereignty
Separation of Powers
Checks and Balances
Federalism
Bill of Rights
Constitution

The Constitution and the Bill of Rights

Across

2. The principle that the government's powers are defined and restricted. (2 words)

3. A system that divides power between national and state governments.

4. A system where each branch of government can limit the powers of the others. (3 words)

5. Fair treatment through the normal judicial system. (2 words)

6. The first ten amendments to the Constitution that protect individual liberties.

8. he principle that the authority of the government comes from the people. (2 words)

9. A change or addition to the Constitution.

10. The foundational document that established the framework for the U.S. government.

Down

1. The division of government responsibilities into distinct branches. (3 words)

7. The state of being free within society from oppressive restrictions.

by 3andB Staff Writer | October 1, 2024

The Birth of a Nation: Navigating the Federalist Era

Think about being tasked with building a brand-new country from the ground up. Where would you start? What challenges would you face? This was precisely the situation George Washington and John Adams found themselves in during the Federalist Era, a crucial period in American history that laid the foundation for the United States we know today. As we explore this pivotal time, we'll uncover how these early leaders shaped the young nation's government, economy, and international relations, setting precedents that continue to influence American politics centuries later.

The Federalist Era established a strong national government under the Constitution, emphasizing federalism and key institutions like the Bank of the United States.

The Washington Presidency: Setting Precedents

When George Washington took office in 1789, he faced the monumental task of turning the Constitution's words into a functioning government. As the first president, his actions would set precedents for all who followed. Washington assembled a talented cabinet, including Alexander Hamilton as Secretary of the Treasury and Thomas Jefferson as Secretary of State, to help navigate the challenges ahead.

One of Washington's most significant contributions was establishing the principle of executive authority. He asserted the president's right to conduct foreign policy, as seen in his Proclamation of Neutrality during the war between Britain and France in 1793. This decision emphasized the president's power in international affairs and set a precedent for American neutrality in European conflicts.

Washington also faced domestic challenges, such as the Whiskey Rebellion of 1794. His decisive action in personally leading troops to quell the uprising demonstrated the federal government's authority to enforce laws and maintain order, a crucial step in solidifying the new nation's stability.

Hamilton's Financial Plan: Building Economic Foundations

Alexander Hamilton, as Secretary of the Treasury, developed a comprehensive financial plan that would shape the American economy for generations.

His plan included three main components:

1. Assumption of state debts: The federal government would take on the Revolutionary

War debts of individual states, strengthening national unity.

2. *Creation of a national bank:* The First Bank of the United States would provide a stable currency and facilitate economic growth.

3. *Protective tariffs:* These would encourage the growth of American manufacturing and generate revenue for the government.

Hamilton's policies laid the groundwork for a strong central government and a robust national economy. However, they also sparked intense debate and opposition, particularly from Thomas Jefferson and James Madison, who feared too much federal power.

The Rise of Political Parties

The disagreements over Hamilton's financial plan and the proper role of the federal government led to the formation of the first political parties in the United States. The Federalists, led by Hamilton, advocated for a strong central government and a commercial economy. In contrast, the Democratic-Republicans, led by Jefferson and Madison, favored a more limited federal government and an agrarian society.

This political divide would shape American politics for decades to come, establishing the two-party system that continues to define U.S. democracy today.

John Adams and the Challenges of the Late 1790s

When John Adams succeeded Washington as president in 1797, he inherited a nation facing both domestic and international challenges. The most pressing issue was deteriorating relations with France, which led to an undeclared naval war known as the Quasi-War.

In response to the perceived threat from France and growing domestic opposition, Adams and the Federalist-controlled Congress passed the Alien and Sedition Acts in 1798. These controversial laws restricted free speech and made it easier to deport foreign residents. The acts were widely criticized as unconstitutional and became a rallying point for the Democratic-Republicans.

Despite these challenges, Adams successfully negotiated an end to the Quasi-War with France, avoiding a full-scale conflict. However, the political divisions that emerged during his presidency would contribute to his defeat in the election of 1800, marking the end of the Federalist Era.

The Federalist Era, encompassing the presidencies of Washington and Adams, was a time of great accomplishment and significant challenges. These early leaders established crucial precedents for executive power, built the foundations of the American economy, and navigated complex international relations. While their actions sometimes sparked controversy, they laid the groundwork for the stable and prosperous nation that would emerge in the 19th century.

As you reflect on this period, consider how the decisions made during the Federalist Era continue to shape American government and politics today. The debates over federal power, economic policy, and the role of political parties that began in this era remain relevant in contemporary discussions about the future of the United States.

16. The Federalist Era: Washington and Adams Presidencies

GUIDED NOTES

I. Key Terms

1. Federalist Era: ____

2. Proclamation of Neutrality: ____________________________________

3. Whiskey Rebellion: ____

4. First Bank of the United States: _______________________________

5. Quasi-War: ____

II. Main Concept Overview

The Federalist Era was a crucial period in American history that _________________ for the United States we know today. During this time, early leaders shaped the young nation's _________________, _________________, and _________________, setting precedents that continue to influence American politics centuries later.

III. Matching Section

Match the person with their role or contribution:

_____ George Washington	A. Secretary of the Treasury, developed a comprehensive financial plan
_____ Alexander Hamilton	B. First President, set precedents for executive authority
_____ Thomas Jefferson	C. President during the Quasi-War with France
_____ John Adams	D. Secretary of State, opposed Hamilton's financial plan
_____ James Madison	E. Collaborated with Jefferson in forming the Democratic-Republican party

IV. Fill in the Table

Complete the table with information about Hamilton's Financial Plan:

Component	Description	Purpose
Assumption of state debts		
Creation of a national bank		
Protective tariffs		

V. True or False

_____ Washington's Proclamation of Neutrality emphasized the president's power in domestic affairs.

_____ The Whiskey Rebellion demonstrated the federal government's authority to enforce laws.

_____ Hamilton's financial plan was universally accepted without any opposition.

_____ The Federalists favored a limited federal government and an agrarian society.

_____ The Alien and Sedition Acts were passed during John Adams' presidency.

VI. Application Question

Explain how the political divisions that emerged during the Federalist Era relate to contemporary debates about the role of the federal government in the United States.

____

____

____

____

____

16. The Federalist Era: Washington and Adams Presidencies - Reflection Questions

1

How might your life be different today if Washington had chosen to become a king or president for life instead of stepping down after two terms?

Consider how this decision shaped the American presidency and democracy. Think about the implications for political power transitions and the balance of power in government.

2

In what ways do you see the debate between Federalists and Democratic-Republicans reflected in current political discussions?

Reflect on contemporary debates about the size and role of the federal government. How do these historical perspectives relate to modern political ideologies?

3

In what ways do you think the precedents set during the Federalist Era have shaped your own understanding of the role of government in society?

Think about your beliefs regarding federal versus state power, the role of the president, and the function of political parties. How might these views be influenced by the decisions made during this formative period of American history?

Scenario 1

Scenario: **School Debt Takeover**

Imagine your high school decides to implement a "Hamilton-inspired" plan. The student government announces it will take on all individual student debts (e.g., lunch money owed, library fines, sports fees) and pay them off using the school's general fund.

a) How might this plan affect school unity and student attitudes toward the student government?
b) What potential problems could arise from this policy? Consider both supporters and opponents.
c) How does this scenario reflect the debates surrounding Hamilton's plan to assume state debts?

Scenario 2

Scenario: **Social Media Sedition Act**

Your school implements a new policy inspired by the Alien and Sedition Acts. It allows for the suspension of students who post negative comments about the school or its staff on social media, citing the need to maintain the school's reputation.

a) How might this policy impact students' freedom of expression and the overall school atmosphere?
b) What arguments could be made for and against this policy? Consider both safety/reputation and individual rights.
c) How does this scenario reflect the debates surrounding the Alien and Sedition Acts during the Federalist Era?

16. The Federalist Era: Washington and Adams Presidencies - Vocabulary

TERM	DEFINITION
Federalist	
Precedent	
Cabinet	
Neutrality	
Assumption	

16. The Federalist Era: Washington and Adams Presidencies - Vocabulary

TERM	DEFINITION
Tariff	
Democratic-Republican	
Quasi-War	
Sedition	
Executive	

The Federalist Era

Y I P E U L P E K G B E A M W A T O E Z X W E Z
H S U F S D M F U Y N H K F K I O D F D P U Y G
F M E G N J K D O S C C G X Z X L E D W K J Q J
O U F D Y X O T T A Z J B K O A Q M C Q Z Z T E
Q K M W I Z G A A F S O J J O T K O X T S U S X
I W P S A T J L X R A G K Y C K F C U R H X X E
A C Z I L A I G B I I F M W W X K R C B P L S C
C M C W U Y M O D V V F W N C B G A T D D I B U
J A W C S U S M N G L H F P Z R P T S L A X T T
I V B X F B U K J J F H X S A V Z I N M N Y K I
V S L I S S V L B W T H T S C Z E C Y O E R A V
O H W O N N M Q T J F L B P T K W R X K U D L E
H D G F E E Z B U N G B N R E Z A E F N T M B V
V S E W T H T O E A B C J V G K S P R Y R I O F
N U R I H B W F M K S Z W Y S T S U M U A V A V
G B I A A G G I J T E I S H N P U B B D L G A O
T C U B H N P B V B Q A W D J S M L W K I O F A
T P R E C E D E N T J Y K A C O P I L K T K G S
K W X Z R I C G N R Q R D K R W T C J U Y U B B
G X I T F H P F V K L U Q L I M I A H V R U Z K
J Q D X R X V A V F L C Y E Y T O N A A V U W G
V G D E F E D E R A L I S T H S N L Z M H U I Z
Y N V D I N N S S J E X Z R R P A F I W C M S O
P A M G U K N S B Y Y Q F G I C J A N V U R C Y

Executive
Sedition
Quasi-War
Democratic-Republican
Tariff
Assumption
Neutrality
Cabinet
Precedent
Federalist

The Federalist Era

Across

2. An action or decision that serves as a guide for future similar circumstances.

3. Relating to the branch of government responsible for enforcing laws.

4. Supporter of a strong central government during the early years of the U.S.

5. An undeclared state of hostilities between nations. (2-words)

6. A tax on imported goods.

7. The act of taking on or taking over something, such as debt.

8. Group of advisors to the president, including department heads.

9. Conduct or speech inciting people to rebel against the authority of a state.

10. State of not taking sides in a conflict between other parties.

Down

1. Member of the political party opposing the Federalists. (2-words)

by 3andB Staff Writer | October 1, 2024

The Birth of American Political Parties: Shaping the Young Republic

The nation is newly formed, its citizens are buzzing with excitement and uncertainty about their future. This was the United States in the late 18th century, fresh from revolution and eager to chart its course. But how would this young country make decisions and govern itself? The answer lay in the formation of political parties, a process that would fundamentally shape American democracy. In this article, we'll explore how the first American political parties emerged, their key differences, and the lasting impact they've had on U.S. politics.

The formation of political parties in the U.S. during the 18th century emerged from differing views on federal power and governance, leading to the rise of the Federalists and Democratic-Republicans.

The Roots of Division

In the early days of the American republic, there was hope that the new nation could avoid the partisan divisions that plagued European politics. George Washington, in his Farewell Address, famously warned against the "baneful effects of the spirit of party." However, even as he spoke these words, the seeds of political parties were already taking root.

The main divide emerged between two groups: the Federalists, led by Alexander Hamilton, and the Democratic-Republicans (also known as the Republicans or Jeffersonians), led by Thomas Jefferson and James Madison. These factions grew out of fundamental disagreements about the role and scope of the federal government.

The Federalist Vision

The Federalists, with Alexander Hamilton at the helm, advocated for a strong central government. They believed this was necessary to:

1. Establish economic stability and growth
2. Maintain order and security
3. Compete effectively on the world stage

Hamilton's financial plan, which included creating a national bank and assuming state debts, was a cornerstone of the Federalist agenda. They argued that a powerful federal government was crucial for building a robust economy and unifying the diverse states into a cohesive nation.

Federalists tended to draw support from urban areas, especially in the Northeast. Their base included merchants, bankers, and wealthy landowners who saw benefits in Hamilton's economic policies.

The Democratic-Republican Alternative

In contrast, the Democratic-Republicans, led by Thomas Jefferson and James Madison, feared that a strong central government might evolve into a monarchy or tyranny. They championed:

1. States' rights and local governance
2. Strict interpretation of the Constitution
3. An agrarian economy and limited industrialization

Jefferson and his allies believed that the best safeguard of liberty was to keep government close to the people. They were suspicious of Hamilton's financial system, seeing it as favoring the wealthy elite at the expense of ordinary citizens.

The Democratic-Republicans found their strongest support among farmers, artisans, and frontier settlers. They appealed to those who valued individual liberty and were wary of concentrated power.

The Impact of Foreign Affairs

The French Revolution and subsequent wars in Europe became a flashpoint for partisan division in America. The Federalists, admiring British political stability and economic ties, favored a pro-British foreign policy. The Democratic-Republicans, inspired by the ideals of the French Revolution, sympathized with France.

This foreign policy split had domestic repercussions. The Federalist-backed Jay's Treaty with Britain in 1794 and the Alien and Sedition Acts of 1798 fueled Democratic-Republican opposition and helped solidify party lines.

The Election of 1800: A Turning Point

The election of 1800, often called the "Revolution of 1800," marked a crucial moment in the development of American political parties. The bitter campaign between John Adams (Federalist) and Thomas Jefferson (Democratic-Republican) highlighted the deep divisions between the two factions.

Jefferson's victory signaled a shift in power and demonstrated that peaceful transfer of power between opposing parties was possible in a republic. This set a vital precedent for American democracy.

Legacy and Evolution

The two-party system that emerged in this era has remained a defining feature of American politics. While the specific parties have changed over time, the basic structure of two dominant, competing parties has endured.

The Federalist Party eventually dissolved, but many of its ideas about strong central government were later adopted by other parties. The Democratic-Republicans evolved into the modern Democratic Party, though its ideology has shifted significantly over time.

The formation of political parties in the early United States was not a planned process, but rather an organic development arising from genuine ideological differences about how the new nation should be governed. These divisions, centered on issues like the power of federal government, economic policy, and foreign relations, continue to shape American political debate today.

Understanding the origins of American political parties provides valuable insight into the nature of U.S. democracy. It reminds us that vigorous debate and disagreement, far from being a flaw in the system, have been integral to American governance from the very beginning. As you consider the political landscape today, remember that you're observing the latest chapter in a story that began with the birth of the nation itself.

17. The Formation of Political Parties

GUIDED NOTES

I. Key Terms

1. Federalists: ______________________________

2. Democratic-Republicans: ______________________________

3. Partisan: ______________________________

II. Main Concept Overview

The formation of political parties in the early United States was a result of ______________________ about how the new nation should be governed. Despite George Washington's warning against the "______________________ of the spirit of party," two main factions emerged: the ______________________ led by Alexander Hamilton, and the ______________________ led by Thomas Jefferson and James Madison.

III. Matching Section

Match each term with its correct description:

_____ Federalists

_____ Democratic-Republicans

_____ Jay's Treaty

_____ Election of 1800

_____ Alien and Sedition Acts

A. Favored states' rights and local governance

B. Drew support from urban areas and wealthy landowners

C. Advocated for a strong central government

D. Fueled partisan division in foreign policy

E. Demonstrated peaceful transfer of power between parties

IV. True or False

_____ The Federalists supported a strict interpretation of the Constitution.

_____ The Democratic-Republicans found their strongest support among farmers and frontier settlers.

_____ Both parties agreed on the best approach to foreign policy regarding France and Britain.

_____ The election of 1800 is often called the "Revolution of 1800".

_____ The two-party system that emerged in this era has remained a defining feature of American politics.

V. Fill in the Table

Complete the table comparing the two main political parties:

Aspect	Federalists	Democratic-Republicans
Leader(s)		
View on Federal Government		
Economic Vision		
Main Supporters		
Foreign Policy Leaning		

VI. Application Question

Describe how the debate over the role and scope of the federal government in the early United States relates to political discussions today. Provide specific examples from the article to support your answer.

____

____

____

____

VII. Reflection/Summary

Summarize the main reasons for the formation of political parties in the early United States and explain their lasting impact on American democracy.

____

____

____

____

17. The Formation of Political Parties - Reflection Questions

1

How might your life be different if political parties had never formed in the United States?

Consider how parties influence elections, policy-making, and public discourse. Think about how you engage with political information and form your opinions. How might this process be different in a system without established parties?

2

If you were a citizen in the early republic, which party would you have been more likely to support, the Federalists or the Democratic-Republicans? Why?

Reflect on your own values and priorities. How do they align with the principles of each party? Consider factors like your hypothetical occupation, location, and economic status in that era.

3

How has the two-party system, established in the early republic, shaped modern American politics? Do you think this system is still effective today?

Think about the benefits and drawbacks of a two-party system. Consider how it affects political discourse, representation, and governance. How might American politics be different with a multi-party system?

Scenario 1

Scenario: The Impact of Social Media on Political Discourse

A new social media platform gains popularity, promising to create "echo chambers" where users only see political content that aligns with their views, potentially deepening political divides.

a) How might this platform affect political discourse and party loyalty?
b) What parallels can you draw between this scenario and the partisan newspapers of the early republic?
c) How could citizens and political leaders work to promote cross-party dialogue in this environment?

Scenario 2

Scenario: The Rise of a Powerful Third Party

Imagine that a new political party gains significant support in the upcoming election, challenging the traditional two-party system. This party claims to represent a middle ground between the current major parties

a) How might this new party's emergence affect the policies and strategies of the existing two major parties?
b) What challenges might this new party face in gaining widespread acceptance and representation?
c) How does this scenario compare to the emergence of the Democratic-Republican party in the early United States?

17. The Formation of Political Parties - Vocabulary

TERM	DEFINITION
Federalists	
Democratic-Republicans	
Partisan	
Faction	
Agrarian	

TERM	DEFINITION
Industrialization	
Diplomacy	
Ideology	
Consensus	
Ratification	

17: WORD SEARCH

The Formation of Political Parties

R A T I F I C A T I O N M C X I K P J Y K R U A

Z E F T Y I U Z I X O A N O N T J V I I N Y X M

V G P V P Z I A J N M F Y N J K S Y N A H E R Z

Q Q G A Q E K P U O Z R M S W V A G R A R I A N

U O A F N I O L Z D P R P E V T H N A L I A K E

R I C F L W Z Z U I S B H N N W B G Z U F X I Q

T O A I T O B V C J R P H S E H Y S N A M B V E

I R P J M A M R I F D R Q U N B N P O X Z T Z T

Y W M F E D E R A L I S T S B D B N N V M R G G

L Z E V M I P A R T I S A N A I P C P N R E L A

T Q W Q M N V O Z N W T O Z B G A K T G E B B T

H Y D D U L L F F Y G D I W A V H E T I U R I D

I N Y E I L F A C T I O N I B E O I G O H S Y T

K G M F Z P B P X L X W L N F T B P K M P Z C O

D D F T M K L M F Q Q X Z I S L Z G O E N O O N

G K I D F D A O D B V F P K D S Y M G E K S G Q

F H L V M H X Y M W P M G C G E X V L D R Q R S

S I N D U S T R I A L I Z A T I O N P N W Q E V

X Z O I L L L F V G C V D L H S R L P Y T B N M

U T G S B G U L T P H Y R X J J X T O P X D S C

M E M G D T I C Z P S Z Z P D D T S S G R Q C V

E G S Z P A O G S V Z F B T R C F M N A Y I Y F

M E S Q Q O Y E V K G P S P D I K Q W X S J J S

Z W D E M O C R A T I C R E P U B L I C A N S C

Ratification

Diplomacy

Faction

Federalists

Consensus

Industrialization

Partisan

Ideology

Agrarian

Democratic-Republicans

The Formation of Political Parties

Across

2. The profession, activity, or skill of managing international relations.

7. Relating to cultivated land or the rural economy.

8. A small, organized, dissenting group within a larger one.

9. General agreement among a group of people.

10. The development of industries in a country on a wide scale.

Down

1. Jefferson's party championing states' rights and limited federal power. (2 words)

3. Hamilton's group advocating for a strong central government.

4. The action of signing or giving formal consent to a treaty, contract, or agreement, making it officially valid.

5. A system of ideas and ideals, especially one which forms the basis of economic or political theory and policy.

6. Strongly supporting a particular party, cause, or person.

18. The Jefferson Era and the Louisiana Purchase

by 3andB Staff Writer | October 1, 2024

The Jefferson Era: Shaping a Young Nation's Destiny

When Thomas Jefferson took office as the third President of the United States in 1801, he ushered in an era of significant change. Jefferson's election marked a shift from the Federalist policies of his predecessors to a new vision of democratic ideals and limited government. But how did Jefferson's presidency impact the young nation, and what role did the Louisiana Purchase play in shaping America's future?

The Jefferson Era featured the Louisiana Purchase in 1803, which doubled the U.S. territory and secured the Mississippi River.

Jefferson's Vision: Democracy and Expansion

Thomas Jefferson believed in a republic of yeoman farmers and sought to limit the power of the federal government. His vision for America included:

1. Reducing government spending and the national debt
2. Promoting agriculture and westward expansion
3. Protecting individual liberties
4. Advancing education and scientific knowledge

These ideals would guide his decisions throughout his presidency and leave a lasting impact on the nation.

The Louisiana Purchase: A Game-Changing Opportunity

In 1803, an unexpected opportunity arose that would dramatically alter the course of American history. France, under Napoleon Bonaparte, offered to sell the Louisiana Territory to the United States. This vast expanse of land stretched from the Mississippi River to the Rocky Mountains, encompassing approximately 828,000 square miles.

Jefferson faced a dilemma. The Constitution didn't explicitly give the president the power to purchase foreign territory. However, the potential benefits were enormous:

- Doubling the size of the United States
- Securing control of the Mississippi River and the port of New Orleans
- Providing room for westward expansion
- Preventing European powers from gaining a foothold in North America

After careful consideration, Jefferson decided to seize this once-in-a-lifetime opportunity. He sent James Monroe and Robert Livingston to negotiate with France, ultimately securing the Louisiana Territory for $15 million – roughly 4 cents per acre in today's currency!

Impact and Legacy of the Louisiana Purchase

The Louisiana Purchase had far-reaching consequences for the United States:

1. *Territorial Expansion:* It doubled the size of the country, providing vast new territories for settlement and development.

2. *Economic Growth:* Access to the Mississippi River and New Orleans boosted trade and commerce.

3. *Native American Relations:* The acquisition led to increased conflicts with indigenous peoples as settlers moved westward.

4. *Slavery Debate:* The new territories raised questions about the expansion of slavery, contributing to tensions that would eventually lead to the Civil War.

5. *Exploration:* It paved the way for the Lewis and Clark Expedition, which mapped much of the new territory and made contact with Native American tribes.

Challenges and Controversies

Despite its benefits, the Jefferson Era was not without challenges:

1. *Barbary Wars:* Jefferson faced his first foreign policy test with piracy in the Mediterranean, leading to the First Barbary War (1801-1805).

2. *Embargo Act of 1807:* In response to British and French interference with American shipping, Jefferson imposed a controversial embargo that hurt the U.S. economy.

3. *Constitutional Debates:* The Louisiana Purchase sparked discussions about the limits of presidential power and constitutional interpretation.

The Jefferson Legacy

Thomas Jefferson's presidency left an indelible mark on American history. His commitment to democratic ideals, coupled with the audacious Louisiana Purchase, set the stage for America's westward expansion and emergence as a continental power.

Today, we can see Jefferson's influence in many aspects of American life:

- The emphasis on individual liberty and limited government
- The importance of education and scientific inquiry
- The idea of America as an "empire of liberty"

As you reflect on the Jefferson Era, consider how decisions made over 200 years ago continue to shape our nation today. How might America be different if Jefferson had not made the Louisiana Purchase? What challenges and opportunities did this massive expansion create for future generations?

The Jefferson Era reminds us that bold actions, guided by strong principles, can have long-lasting impacts on a nation's destiny. As you continue to study American history, keep in mind how the decisions of the past have shaped the present – and how your generation's choices will influence the future.

18. The Jefferson Era and the Louisiana Purchase

GUIDED NOTES

I. Key Terms

1. Yeoman farmers: ______________________________

2. Louisiana Territory: ______________________________

3. Embargo Act: ______________________________

II. Main Concept Overview

Thomas Jefferson became the ____________ President of the United States in ____________. His election marked a shift from ____________________ policies to a new vision of _______________ ideals and ________________ government.

III. Jefferson's Vision (Fill in the blank)

1. Reducing _______________ spending and the national _______________

2. Promoting _______________ and westward _______________

3. Protecting individual _______________

4. Advancing _______________ and scientific knowledge

IV. The Louisiana Purchase

A. Year of purchase: __________

B. Size of territory: approximately ________________ square miles

C. Cost: $_________________

D. Price per acre (in today's currency): ________________

V. Match each consequence of the Louisiana Purchase with its description:

_____ Territorial Expansion	A. Boosted trade and commerce
_____ Economic Growth	B. Mapped much of the new territory
_____ Native American Relations	C. Doubled the size of the country
_____ Slavery Debate	D. Raised questions about expansion of slavery
_____ Exploration	E. Led to increased conflicts with indigenous peoples

VI. True or False

_____ The Constitution explicitly gave the president power to purchase foreign territory.

_____ The Louisiana Purchase provided access to the Mississippi River and the port of New Orleans.

_____ Jefferson's Embargo Act of 1807 helped the U.S. economy.

_____ The Louisiana Purchase paved the way for the Lewis and Clark Expedition.

_____ The First Barbary War was fought in the Mediterranean.

VII. Fill in the Table: Challenges during the Jefferson Era

Challenge	Years	Main Issue
Barbary Wars		
Embargo Act		
Constitutional Debates		

VIII. Application Question

How did the Louisiana Purchase align with Jefferson's vision for America? Provide specific examples from the article to support your answer.

____

____

____

IX. Reflection/Summary

In your own words, summarize the main impacts of the Jefferson Era and the Louisiana Purchase on American history. How do you think these events continue to shape the United States today?

____

____

____

18. The Jefferson Era and the Louisiana Purchase - Reflection Questions

1

How might your life be different today if the Louisiana Purchase had never occurred?

Consider how the geography, economy, and culture of the United States might have developed differently without this massive territorial expansion. Think about where you live and how that area might have been affected.

2

In what ways do you see Jefferson's vision of "limited government" reflected in current political debates?

Reflect on recent news stories or discussions you've heard about the role of government in people's lives. How do these debates echo or differ from Jefferson's ideals?

3

How do you think the Louisiana Purchase and subsequent westward expansion affected your family's history?

Consider your family's background and any stories you might know about their migration or settlement patterns. How might your family's story have been different without this expansion?

Scenario 1

Scenario: What if France had refused to sell the Louisiana Territory?
Imagine that Napoleon Bonaparte decided to keep the Louisiana Territory as part of France's empire in the Americas. In 1804, France begins to heavily colonize the region, establishing new cities and trading posts along the Mississippi River.

a) How might this have affected the United States' westward expansion?
b) What potential conflicts could have arisen between the U.S. and France?
c) How might this scenario have influenced the future development of Native American tribes in the region?

Scenario 2

Scenario: What if the Lewis and Clark expedition had failed?
Imagine that the Lewis and Clark expedition encountered insurmountable challenges and was forced to turn back before reaching the Pacific. They return with limited information about the Louisiana Territory and its indigenous inhabitants.

a) How might this have affected American understanding and settlement of the West?
b) What impact could this have had on relations with Native American tribes in the region?
c) How might this failure have influenced future government-sponsored explorations and scientific endeavors?

18. The Jefferson Era and the Louisiana Purchase - Vocabulary

TERM	DEFINITION
Barbary Wars	
Embargo	
Expansion	
Jefferson	
Liberty	

TERM	DEFINITION
Louisiana	
Mississippi	
Napoleon	
Republic	
Territory	

The Jefferson Era and the Louisiana Purchase

```
E U W C Y N G C P Y A T G O W P K E M G K K Y R
T B M L D T S Z G K O N H M L I C M M W V D S C
S G E G A O O X K V K O U O M P Q L P B C Y R X
H Z T J I V A Z R J K M D M Y V J O Z W A B F X
C Q X Z E M F N D B H M L B R P G N Y M B R W R
R Z Q W M F V O D M O G Q C D E U S C K J C G F
L Z W C Z L F Q J K Q N A U S N P G A Z V H K O
W M O E V W R E T V H G T Q J U M U L A F M R D
S G L F D Y G Z R C T H D I B T U T B P R D N T
V L O B G O M I S S I S S I P P I Q M L E F W U
Y T U F C S L R C I O V B D R D O I X C I B E H
Y E I W M G I I N T B N F E N I A G M O S C M P
G R S N B J K F B K Y H Z S G Z U Z L U X Y M P
G R I Q Q W Y Z H E A T V M W X D L M T V R C V
F I A G Y X M B C K R S K C D I Z P I I X Y M Z
F T N H Y W T E P Z F T K S D J E E W Z T O J Q
Z O A Q E M Z J J L D Y Y M G C X K M Y W Y D A
T R Q K O N L S O H P K M T U N A P O L E O N Z
L Y G W H U L I I O B I E D G O Y X V H A Z Q J
L G X B P N R Y T A E H B D Q Z Y K R H E J U T
X R B A R B A R Y W A R S P J E G R H P L H Z H
O A S N W W U V Z M J J J O D A A R T J U E R L
D M T Z P W Y Q F Y U W R U C H E M U G E R K C
I M F W Q Y U C H I K E S K A Q F L X V F U R Y
```

Territory	Republic	Napoleon
Mississippi	Louisiana	Liberty
Jefferson	Embargo	Barbary Wars

The Jefferson Era and the Louisiana Purchase

Across

3. The form of government Jefferson envisioned, centered on citizen farmers.

4. A crucial river secured for American use through Jefferson's land deal.

5. Jefferson's first foreign policy test involving Mediterranean pirates. (2 words)

6. The French leader who sold a large territory to the United States.

8. A core value in Jefferson's vision for America, emphasizing personal freedom.

9. A large area of land, like the one Jefferson acquired from France.

Down

1. The vast territory purchased during Jefferson's presidency.

2. The third U.S. President who orchestrated a major land acquisition.

7. The growth of U.S. territory, dramatically accelerated by Jefferson's actions.

by 3andB Staff Writer | October 1, 2024

The War of 1812 and Its Aftermath: A Turning Point in American History

Imagine a young nation, barely three decades old, facing off against one of the world's superpowers. This was the United States in 1812, squaring up to Great Britain in a conflict that would shape the course of American history. The War of 1812, often called the "Second War of Independence," was a pivotal moment that tested the resilience of the fledgling republic and set the stage for its future growth and development. In this article, we'll explore the causes, key events, and lasting impacts of this crucial chapter in American history.

The War of 1812, fought between the United States and Britain, ended in a stalemate but bolstered American nationalism and led to the decline of the Federalist Party.

The Road to War: Tensions on the High Seas

At the dawn of the 19th century, the United States found itself caught in the crossfire of a much larger conflict between Britain and France. As these European powers battled for supremacy, American ships became easy targets. The British, in particular, were notorious for impressing American sailors – forcibly recruiting them into the Royal Navy. This practice, along with trade restrictions, fueled growing resentment in the United States.

The Push for Expansion

While maritime issues were a major concern, land also played a crucial role in the build-up to war. Many Americans, especially those in the Western frontier, eyed British-controlled Canada with interest. Some saw an opportunity for territorial expansion, while others worried about British support for Native American tribes resisting American settlement.

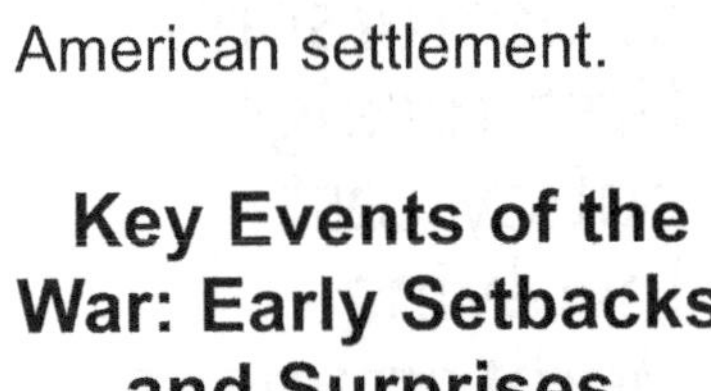

Key Events of the War: Early Setbacks and Surprises

When war was declared in June 1812, many Americans expected a quick victory. However, the initial attempts to invade Canada ended in embarrassing failure. The U.S. was unprepared for war, with a small army and navy facing off against the battle-hardened British forces.

Yet, there were surprising American successes at sea. The USS Constitution, nicknamed "Old Ironsides," famously defeated several British warships, boosting American morale and proving that the young nation could hold its own against the world's premier naval power.

The Burning of Washington and the Star-Spangled Banner

In August 1814, the war took a dramatic turn when British forces invaded Washington D.C., burning several public buildings, including the White House. This shocking event was followed by an attack on Baltimore, where American forces successfully defended Fort McHenry. It was during this battle that Francis Scott Key wrote the poem that would become "The Star-Spangled Banner," the future national anthem.

The Battle of New Orleans

The final major battle of the war took place in New Orleans in January 1815. Led by future president Andrew Jackson, American forces achieved a decisive victory over the British. Ironically, the battle occurred after the peace treaty had been signed but before news had reached the combatants, highlighting the slow communication of the era.

The Treaty of Ghent and Its Aftermath

The war officially ended with the Treaty of Ghent, signed on December 24, 1814. Surprisingly, the treaty essentially returned things to how they were before the war, with no major territorial changes. However, the conflict's aftermath had far-reaching consequences for the United States:

1. National Pride: Despite the lack of clear military victory, Americans celebrated the war's end with a surge of patriotism. The young nation had stood up to a global superpower and survived, boosting national confidence.

2. Native American Relations: The war dealt a severe blow to Native American resistance in the Northwest Territory, paving the way for further westward expansion.

3. Economic Changes: The war spurred American manufacturing as the British naval blockade cut off European imports, encouraging domestic production.

4. Political Shifts: The Federalist Party, which had opposed the war, fell into decline, ushering in the "Era of Good Feelings" under a one-party system led by the Democratic-Republicans.

5. Foreign Policy: The war marked the beginning of a long period of peace between the U.S. and Britain, eventually leading to a strong alliance.

The War of 1812 may not have resulted in major territorial gains, but its impact on the American psyche and the nation's development was profound. It solidified the United States' independence, spurred economic growth, and set the stage for the country's expansion and rise as a global power. As you reflect on this pivotal moment in history, consider how the echoes of 1812 still resonate in America's national identity and its place on the world stage today.

Interesting Fact

The White House got its name after being painted white to cover scorch marks from British attacks in 1814.

19. The War of 1812 and Its Aftermath

GUIDED NOTES

I. Key Terms

1. Impressment: ____
2. Treaty of Ghent: ____
3. USS Constitution: _______________________________________

II. Main Concept Overview

The War of 1812 is often called the "__________________________" because it tested the resilience of the young United States against ____________________ ____________. This conflict had far-reaching consequences for the United States, including impacts on __________________________, ____________________ ____________, and __________________________.

III. Matching Section

Match each term with its correct description:

_____ Francis Scott Key	A. Wrote the poem that became "The Star-Spangled Banner"
_____ Andrew Jackson	B. Led American forces to victory at the Battle of New Orleans
_____ "Old Ironsides"	C. Nickname for the USS Constitution
_____ Federalist Party	D. Political party that fell into decline after the war
_____ Washington D.C.	E. City where British forces burned several public buildings

IV. True or False

_____ The War of 1812 resulted in major territorial changes.

_____ The Battle of New Orleans took place after the peace treaty had been signed.

_____ The war dealt a severe blow to Native American resistance in the Northwest Territory.

_____ The war spurred American manufacturing as the British naval blockade cut off European imports.

_____ The war marked the beginning of a long period of conflict between the U.S. and Britain.

V. Application Question

Describe how the War of 1812 affected American national pride. Use specific examples from the article to support your answer.

VII. Reflection/Summary

In your own words, summarize the main impacts of the War of 1812 on the United States. How did this conflict influence the nation's development?

19. The War of 1812 and Its Aftermath - Reflection Questions

1

How might your life be different today if the United States had lost the War of 1812?

Consider how a British victory might have affected American independence, territorial expansion, and economic development. Think about specific aspects of your daily life, from the language you speak to the territory you live in, that could have been impacted.

2

In what ways do you see the legacy of the War of 1812 in modern American culture and politics?

Reflect on national symbols like the Star-Spangled Banner, political attitudes towards foreign policy, or the relationship between the U.S. and Britain today. How do these connect to events or outcomes of the War of 1812?

3

If you were a young person living in America in 1812, how would you have felt about the prospect of war with Britain?

Think about the different perspectives of someone living in a coastal city, a frontier settlement, or a Southern plantation. Consider factors like age, occupation, and regional interests that might have influenced your view of the conflict.

Scenario 1

What if the British had successfully defended Canada from American invasion attempts?

Scenario: Imagine that the British and Canadian forces had not only repelled American invasions but also launched a successful counteroffensive, capturing and holding significant portions of the northern United States.

a) How might this outcome have affected the balance of power in North America?
b) What impact could this have had on American expansion westward?
c) How might this have influenced relations between the U.S. and Britain in the following decades?

Scenario 2

What if the USS Constitution had been defeated in its naval battles?

Scenario: Consider a situation where the USS Constitution, instead of earning its "Old Ironsides" nickname through victories, had been soundly defeated by British warships early in the conflict.

a) How might this have affected American morale and the public's support for the war?
b) What impact could this have had on the development of the U.S. Navy?
c) How might this have influenced America's future maritime policies and naval strategies?

19. The War of 1812 and Its Aftermath - Vocabulary

TERM	DEFINITION
Impressment	
Superpowers	
Expansion	
Constitution	
Anthem	

TERM	DEFINITION
Treaty	
Invasion	
Blockade	
Morale	
Patriotism	

The War of 1812 and Its Aftermath

```
N V Y P Y E P B D Y I V I N P B F H C H O V S X
H E E A G J I U G Z R A L T W B Z T B N H X F M
L M S X L V X I R U M Y R Y R E X U P W T C P F
I M P R E S S M E N T C W B G J X Q Y L N S A F
C F S U P E R P O W E R S G O R E X Q Y S W T Q
X A J D C Z B M X J M S I O U U C U N F Z M R R
A O C T G K S H E A M B T T A L O K R I P I I T
D O I L J F W F I L B A L E J I N B N L Q S O R
N D P W F U X I T M H Q X H A W S N T P U H T E
Y B D Z O X X M A L X I Q Y C N T S J J M I I A
E B L O C K A D E K C V Z Q G E I S F N T D S T
P B L O I Q P Q V A Z S T U T X T B S W A L M Y
X O M D N A T F G U D P M J L P U D B N Z O R I
E I S W V H T F Z H F Y O E U A T L P U T H T F
I D R Q A G X O K I P X R A Q N I A M X A J Q F
T U Y Y S I K W V I Y L A W K S O G L Y F X B S
I T J T I N D D I Y A T L Y Y I N X M X G M J R
H O Y D O W W I J E U N E M H O W M F W T E F R
S C S E N M R Y Z M H X T P J N I T E Q N X M R
R J K W X D U X J B P B I H U D D Q Z A X M X O
M A O L W V W Y V N A Y V R E R Q M A D I U U I
Z W J S O W H Y W O M P L Y T M C D X N E I L F
T L A N R H B C J M D X L G X S C P E S T M E E
X Q D A E Y U C J F G K T R N L P D D M J U N A
```

Patriotism
Morale
Blockade
Invasion
Treaty
Anthem
Constitution
Expansion
Superpowers
Impressment

The War of 1812 and Its Aftermath

Across

2. The confidence, enthusiasm, and discipline of a group.

7. British practice of forcing American sailors into their navy.

9. USS ____, nicknamed "Old Ironsides".

10. Very powerful and influential nations.

Down

1. A military operation to prevent access to an area by sea.

3. American desire for territorial ____ was a cause of the war.

4. An armed forces' entry into a country or region to conquer.

5. A formal agreement between nations.

6. "The Star-Spangled Banner" became this after the war.

8. Love for or devotion to one's country.

20. The Monroe Doctrine and Foreign Policy

by 3andB Staff Writer | October 1, 2024

The Monroe Doctrine: Shaping America's Foreign Policy

Think about a young nation, barely out of its teens, boldly declaring to the world's superpowers: "Hands off the Americas!" This is essentially what happened in 1823 when President James Monroe introduced what would become known as the Monroe Doctrine. This pivotal moment in U.S. history not only shaped America's foreign policy for decades to come but also signaled the country's emergence as a player on the world stage. In this article, we'll explore the Monroe Doctrine, its origins, and its lasting impact on American foreign relations.

The Birth of the Monroe Doctrine

In the early 19th century, the United States was a fledgling nation, having gained independence from Britain just a few decades earlier. Meanwhile, many Latin American countries were fighting their own battles for independence from European colonial powers. President James Monroe and his Secretary of State, John Quincy Adams, saw an opportunity to protect American interests and support the newly independent nations to the south.

On December 2, 1823, in his annual message to Congress, President Monroe outlined what would become known as the Monroe Doctrine.

This policy statement contained three key principles:

1. The Americas were no longer open for European colonization.
2. The United States would stay out of European affairs.
3. Any attempt by European powers to interfere in the Americas would be seen as an act of aggression requiring U.S. intervention.

The Context Behind the Doctrine

To understand the Monroe Doctrine, we need to consider the global landscape of the time:

- The United States was wary of European powers regaining control in the Americas.
- Many Latin American countries had recently gained independence and were vulnerable to re-colonization.
- The Russian Empire was expanding its presence in North America, particularly in Alaska and along the Pacific Coast.
- The Holy Alliance (Russia, Prussia, and Austria) was considering helping Spain reclaim its former colonies in Latin America.

These factors created a perfect storm that prompted the U.S. to take a stand and assert its influence in the Western Hemisphere.

Impact and Evolution of the Monroe Doctrine

Initially, the Monroe Doctrine was more symbolic than practical. The young United States lacked the military might to enforce it, and it relied heavily on British naval power to deter European intervention in the Americas. However, as the U.S. grew stronger, the doctrine became a cornerstone of American foreign policy.

Over time, different presidents interpreted and applied the Monroe Doctrine in various ways:

- The Roosevelt Corollary (1904): President Theodore Roosevelt expanded the doctrine, asserting the U.S. right to intervene in Latin American countries to maintain stability and protect American interests.
- The Good Neighbor Policy (1933): President Franklin D. Roosevelt sought to improve relations with Latin American nations by emphasizing cooperation rather than intervention.
- The Cold War Era: The doctrine was used to justify U.S. actions against communist influence in the Western Hemisphere, such as the Cuban Missile Crisis.

Relevance and Criticism

The Monroe Doctrine has been both praised and criticized throughout history. Supporters argue that it protected newly independent Latin American nations from European re-colonization and allowed the United States to assert its role as a world power. Critics, however, point out that it led to a paternalistic attitude towards Latin America and was sometimes used to justify U.S. intervention in the affairs of sovereign nations.

Today, the principles of the Monroe Doctrine continue to influence U.S. foreign policy, albeit in more subtle ways. The idea of the Western Hemisphere as a U.S. sphere of influence remains a part of American strategic thinking, even as global power dynamics shift in the 21st century.

The Monroe Doctrine marked a defining moment in American history, signaling the United States' emergence as a significant player in international affairs. By understanding this pivotal policy, we gain insight into the roots of American foreign relations and the complex interplay between idealism and self-interest that continues to shape U.S. interactions with the world today.

Did You Know?

The term "Monroe Doctrine" wasn't actually used until 1850, almost 30 years after Monroe's original speech. It was coined by journalist John O'Sullivan, the same person who popularized the concept of "Manifest Destiny."

The Monroe Doctrine asserted that the Americas were off-limits to further European colonization and interference.

20. The Monroe Doctrine and Foreign Policy

GUIDED NOTES

I. Key Terms

1. Monroe Doctrine: ______________________________
2. James Monroe: ______________________________
3. John Quincy Adams: ______________________________
4. European colonization: ______________________________
5. Roosevelt Corollary: ______________________________

II. Main Concept Overview

The Monroe Doctrine was a foreign policy statement made by President ______________________ in the year _________. It was primarily aimed at preventing ____________________ powers from further colonizing or interfering in the ______________________.

III. Matching Section

Match the term with its correct description:

_____ Monroe Doctrine	A. Expanded the Monroe Doctrine, asserting U.S. right to intervene in Latin America
_____ Roosevelt Corollary	B. Sought to improve relations with Latin American nations through cooperation
_____ Good Neighbor Policy	C. Declared the Americas off-limits to European colonization
_____ Latin American countries	D. President who introduced the doctrine
_____ James Monroe	E. Many of these were fighting for independence in the early 19th century

IV. Fill in the Table

Principle & Description
The Americas were no longer open for __________________ colonization.
The United States would ________________________________.
Any attempt by European powers to interfere in the Americas would be seen as ___________________________.

V. True or False

_____ The Monroe Doctrine was immediately enforceable by the United States military.

_____ The doctrine was initially more symbolic than practical.

_____ The Monroe Doctrine led to improved relations with European powers.

_____ The doctrine has been both praised and criticized throughout history.

_____ The term "Monroe Doctrine" was coined by James Monroe himself.

VI. Application Question

Describe how the Monroe Doctrine evolved over time, citing at least two specific examples from different time periods mentioned in the article.

____

____

____

____

VII. Reflection/Summary

In your own words, summarize the main points of the Monroe Doctrine and its significance in shaping U.S. foreign policy. How do you think this historical policy might still influence America's role in the world today?

____

____

____

____

20. The Monroe Doctrine and Foreign Policy - Reflection Questions

1

How might your life be different today if the Monroe Doctrine had never been established?

Think about the geopolitical landscape of the Americas. Consider how European influence might have shaped the development of countries in North and South America differently.

2

In what ways do you think the principles of the Monroe Doctrine still influence U.S. foreign policy today?

Reflect on recent international events or conflicts involving the United States and countries in the Western Hemisphere. How might the spirit of the Monroe Doctrine be evident in these situations?

3

How do you think the Monroe Doctrine might be viewed differently if it were introduced in today's globalized world?

Consider the changes in international relations, technology, and global power dynamics since the 1820s. How might these factors affect the reception and implementation of such a policy today?

Scenario 1

Scenario: Social Media Influence

Scenario: A popular European social media company offers free, unlimited data plans to all high school students in Mexico and Central America. In exchange, the company gets exclusive rights to all user data and can influence what news and information these students see.

a) How is this situation similar to the kind of foreign influence the Monroe Doctrine tried to prevent?
b) If you were the U.S. President, how might you respond to this offer from the European company?
c) What could be some positive and negative effects of this deal for the students in Mexico and Central America?

Scenario 2

Scenario: Online Gaming Tournament

Scenario: A major Chinese tech company announces a huge online gaming tournament for all high school students in North and South America. The prizes include college scholarships and high-tech computers. To participate, students must use the company's special game console that collects data on their playing habits and online activities.

a) How might this gaming tournament be seen as a modern version of the foreign influence the Monroe Doctrine was concerned about?
b) What could be some reasons for the U.S. government to be worried about this tournament?
c) If you were invited to participate in this tournament, would you? What factors would you consider in making your decision?

20. The Monroe Doctrine and Foreign Policy - Vocabulary

TERM	DEFINITION
Doctrine	
Intervention	
Foreign policy	
Symbolic	
Corollary	

TERM	DEFINITION
Implications	
Hemisphere	
Influence	
Principles	
Paternalistic	

The Monroe Doctrine and Early American Foreign Policy

F E Q G T S Y M B O L I C M F G S X Z V K J C M
Q U A T D O C T R I N E M Q S G B R R W L K K Q
X Z F Y Y J U O E N I Y Y M Q K M T K F J C Y C
O S O M A Q K V D L A Z G T A U V C H E G L J O
C L R H G X S J C S L G F B U L C J F D H A P N
Q P E Z Y M E I C L Y C I O H L M X Y X H E W I
O Y I C C P R D N T X V E E I H U I A C O Q F M
D S G W P A M H S F P X Z G Q Q N Z A O K C W P
D S N L X T E U K W L H Z U O O G J F R H E G L
D B P P P E Q F N P S U E P J J Z Y K O U X E I
L M O P T R U F E K V X E D V H B M E L Z J T C
O N L O T N D L N G T M V N T K A O G L F M X A
P P I P A A C T G T H B N Q C K R K L A O V M T
I U C A R L H N D N G E L V E E Z N Z R Z G A I
H J Y R D I I M J N K C M E U H A A L Y J D S O
N L C U J S N Q N L V K B I N E S I M A Y W H N
K M X U O T H C P W Q U Z C S S U K N I K W T S
K O D Q K I Y H I G O U F B W P J O E A L Y O I
Y W D U D C A P W P I X D M M R H L J M Y A X B
Q M G L G F O L V P L W K L W A G E R O R P C W
I A C O V M T B U P F E J J R M O R R W X U C I
I L G I S O I Q G G P I S L X J G J T E O E U W
X H B L Z A I N T E R V E N T I O N O D U M P E
A N H T B I S C X S P Y W B H W Z M X F C E R H

Paternalistic

Principles

Influence

Hemisphere

Implications

Corollary

Symbolic

Foreign policy

Intervention

Doctrine

The Monroe Doctrine and Early American Foreign Policy

Across

3. The action of becoming involved in a situation, especially in foreign affairs.
7. Relating to or characterized by the restriction of the freedom and responsibilities of subordinates or dependents in their supposed interest.
8. Half of the earth, especially a half of the earth as divided into northern and southern halves by the equator.
9. The conclusions that can be drawn from something, although not explicitly stated.
10. A proposition that follows from one already proved, like Roosevelt's addition to the Monroe Doctrine.

Down

1. Fundamental truths or propositions that serve as the foundation for a system of belief or behavior.
2. Serving as a symbol, which the Monroe Doctrine initially was due to lack of military power to enforce it.
4. A government's strategy in dealing with other nations, of which the Monroe Doctrine was a key part. (2 words)
5. A stated principle of government policy, formally declared by President Monroe.
6. The capacity to have an effect on the character, development, or behavior of someone or something.

The Path of Expansion: Manifest Destiny and America's Territorial Growth

In the mid-19th century, a powerful idea swept across the United States, shaping its future and forever altering the North American landscape. This concept, known as Manifest Destiny, would drive the young nation to expand westward, reshaping not only its borders but also its identity and place in the world.

The Birth of a Destiny

Manifest Destiny was the belief that the United States was destined—by God, according to some—to expand its dominion and spread democracy and capitalism across the North American continent. This idea, first articulated in 1845 by newspaper editor John L. O'Sullivan, captured the imagination of many Americans and became a driving force behind the country's territorial expansion.

Manifest Destiny was the 19th-century belief that the expansion of the United States across the American continents was both justified and inevitable.

The concept of Manifest Destiny was rooted in several key beliefs:

1. The superiority of American institutions and culture
2. The mission to spread these ideals across the continent
3. The divine right and duty to accomplish this expansion

These beliefs fueled a sense of righteousness and inevitability about American expansion, encouraging settlers, politicians, and adventurers to push ever westward.

Territorial Acquisitions

The era of Manifest Destiny saw the United States grow dramatically in size and power. Several key acquisitions marked this period of expansion:

1. The Louisiana Purchase (1803): Though predating the term "Manifest Destiny," this massive land deal with France doubled the size of the United States and set the stage for westward expansion.

2. Texas Annexation (1845): After gaining independence from Mexico, Texas was annexed by the United States, sparking tensions that would lead to war.

3. Oregon Territory (1846): The Oregon Treaty with Great Britain secured the Pacific Northwest for the United States, extending American territory to the Pacific Ocean.

4. Mexican Cession (1848): Following the Mexican-American War, Mexico ceded a vast area of the Southwest to the United States, including California and parts of New Mexico, Arizona, and Nevada.

5. Gadsden Purchase (1853): This final acquisition from Mexico completed the continental United States as we know it today, adding southern Arizona and New Mexico.

Impact and Consequences

The rapid expansion driven by Manifest Destiny had profound and far-reaching consequences:

1. Native American Displacement: As settlers moved west, Native American tribes were forcibly relocated or confined to reservations, leading to the loss of land, culture, and lives.

2. Economic Growth: New territories provided abundant natural resources and agricultural land, fueling economic development.

3. Sectional Tensions: The question of whether new territories would be slave states or free states intensified divisions between North and South, contributing to the Civil War.

4. National Identity: The idea of Manifest Destiny became intertwined with American exceptionalism, shaping the nation's self-image and foreign policy for generations.

Legacy and Reflection

Today, the concept of Manifest Destiny is viewed more critically. While it led to the creation of the continental United States we know today, it also resulted in the displacement and suffering of Native Americans and contributed to a war with Mexico. The idea's legacy can still be seen in debates about American exceptionalism and the country's role in the world.

As you consider Manifest Destiny, reflect on these questions:

- How did this idea shape American history and identity?
- What were the ethical implications of territorial expansion?
- How does the legacy of Manifest Destiny continue to influence American society and foreign policy today?

Understanding Manifest Destiny and its impact is crucial for grasping the complexities of American history and the forces that shaped the nation. As you continue your studies, consider how this period of expansion set the stage for future developments in American politics, society, and international relations.

21. Manifest Destiny and Territorial Growth

GUIDED NOTES

I. Key Terms

1. Manifest Destiny: ______________________________

2. John L. O'Sullivan: ______________________________

3. Territorial acquisitions: ______________________________

II. Main Concept Overview

Manifest Destiny was a belief that shaped American ____________________ in the mid-19th century.

It asserted that the United States was destined to expand across the ____________________ continent, from the ____________________ Ocean to the ____________________ Ocean.

III. Matching Section

Match the following territorial acquisitions with their descriptions:

_____ Louisiana Purchase	A. Completed the continental United States
_____ Texas Annexation	B. Secured the Pacific Northwest for the U.S.
_____ Oregon Territory	C. Doubled the size of the United States
_____ Mexican Cession	D. Added southern Arizona and New Mexico
_____ Gadsden Purchase	E. Added California and parts of the Southwest

IV. Fill in the Table

Complete the table with information about the key beliefs underlying Manifest Destiny:

Belief & Description
1.
2.
3.

V. True/False

______ The concept of Manifest Destiny was first articulated in 1845.

______ The Louisiana Purchase predated the term "Manifest Destiny."

______ Manifest Destiny contributed to sectional tensions between North and South.

______ Manifest Destiny led to the displacement of Native American tribes.

______ The legacy of Manifest Destiny is viewed uncritically today.

VI. Impact and Consequences

List three consequences of the rapid expansion driven by Manifest Destiny:

1. ______________________________

2. ______________________________

3. ______________________________

VII. Reflection/Summary

Based on the article, how did Manifest Destiny shape American history and identity? How does its legacy continue to influence American society and foreign policy today?

____

____

____

____

21. Manifest Destiny and Territorial Growth - Reflection Questions

1

How do you think the idea of Manifest Destiny influenced individual settlers' decisions to move westward?

Consider the motivations that might have driven people to leave their homes and venture into unknown territories. Think about how the belief in a divine right or duty might have affected their choices and actions.

2

How do you think the rapid territorial expansion affected the development of American identity and values?

Think about how acquiring new lands and resources might have shaped Americans' view of their country and its place in the world. Consider both positive and negative impacts on national character and ideals.

3

Can you draw any parallels between the ideology of Manifest Destiny and modern American foreign policy?

Consider how the ideas of spreading democracy or American values might relate to past expansionist ideals. Think about current international relations and whether you see any echoes of Manifest Destiny in today's policies.

Scenario 1

Scenario: What if the concept of Manifest Destiny had never gained popularity in the United States?

Imagine that the idea of Manifest Destiny never took hold in American culture and politics. The Louisiana Purchase has occurred, but there is no widespread belief in the divine right to expand across the continent.

a) How might this have affected American territorial expansion in the 19th century?
b) How could the absence of Manifest Destiny have influenced the development of American foreign policy today?
c) In what ways might current debates about immigration and border policies be different if the U.S. had not expanded as extensively?

Scenario 2

Scenario: What if the ideology of Manifest Destiny were applied to space exploration today?

Consider a scenario where the spirit of Manifest Destiny is channeled into a aggressive space colonization program in the 21st century.

a) How might this modern “Space Destiny” affect international relations and space treaties?
b) What ethical considerations would arise from applying Manifest Destiny ideas to space exploration and potential extraterrestrial encounters?
c) How could such a program impact current issues on Earth, such as climate change or resource allocation?

21. Manifest Destiny and Territorial Growth - Vocabulary

TERM	DEFINITION
Manifest Destiny	
Expansion	
Acquisition	
Annexation	
Cession	

TERM	DEFINITION
Displacement	
Exceptionalism	
Sectional	
Continental	
Westward	

Manifest Destiny and Territorial Growth

```
Q H H T U D N I P P U D S S V W H E L D G X V I
F J I S D F Y X M X K F J Z O Y T V Y I L A B B
F M A N I F E S T D E S T I N Y A B F S U Q C W
A G A D E X C E P T I O N A L I S M B P M H S A
Y T C T D R K C X D J K C O V E B X J L M Y D M
Z J L Z P U U T X D A C C X B K S K U A T E U R
G J C H O W O I F T T V A E Z H J C E C Z X V V
R A N H D Q C O E F Y A I C W J F F K E N P K L
A V V E G C F N Y A D L M K Q D X F J M V A B X
R W A Y J O T A Y N J M A I T U N Q U E Z N G L
W P E B A O X L Q N Z A H D Y D I P S N X S Q I
I O D S S J C T G E G S T C F Y P S R T W I T A
O Z S M T P A K L X Q H C E K T F F I V H O N X
B H T X R W G F Z A F W L O F Z E J A T W N O Q
D E Q A H W A H N T G J L F N Z R E F J I N F H
M G H D A I Y R Q I H M F O N T C H D S I O W V
J X N B C D B J D O B P X X K V I S U M O P N A
J P K B A O L M H N A S B J N L C N H H O Y Q C
E Y Y O X L K B H A I L Z S C I Q S E K L E J I
C R S F C M Q N C E C N B L R Q F Z N N P U S X
M B P B K Q R W F B O H W R D G F J L V T A Z J
P L H J C A J E J H U B G C V I Y F U V Z A Q A
C E S S I O N S F P L Z Q D D Z G Q E J R N L C
V O M W M B I W Z O O N F P M K Y M N M E A V Z
```

Westward	Continental	Sectional
Exceptionalism	Displacement	Cession
Annexation	Acquisition	Expansion
Manifest Destiny		

Manifest Destiny and Territorial Growth

Across

2. The addition of territory to one's own.

3. Relating to or affecting a particular section or region.

6. The act of becoming larger or more extensive.

7. In a direction toward the west.

8. Forced removal of people from their homes or lands.

10. The act of gaining possession of something.

Down

1. Belief that a country, society, or group is special or superior.

4. 19th-century belief in America's continental expansion. (2 words)

5. Relating to or characteristic of a continent.

9. The act of giving up something, especially land or rights.

22. The Mexican-American War

by 3andB Staff Writer | October 1, 2024

The Mexican-American War: A Pivotal Moment in U.S. History

On the banks of the Rio Grande in 1846, tensions between two nations erupt into a full-scale conflict. This was the reality for many Americans and Mexicans at the start of the Mexican-American War, a conflict that would reshape the map of North America and set the stage for future national debates. In this article, we'll explore the causes, key events, and lasting impact of this pivotal war in U.S. history.

The Seeds of Conflict

The Mexican-American War didn't happen overnight. Its roots can be traced back to the concept of Manifest Destiny, the belief that the United States was destined to expand across the North American continent. This idea fueled American ambitions to acquire new territories, including those belonging to Mexico.

The Mexican-American War (1846-1848) resulted in significant U.S. land gains, including California and New Mexico.

The immediate trigger for the war was the annexation of Texas by the United States in 1845. Texas had declared independence from Mexico in 1836, but Mexico had never recognized this claim. The situation escalated when a dispute arose over the southern border of Texas. The U.S. claimed it was the Rio Grande, while Mexico insisted it was the Nueces River, further north.

The War Begins

In April 1846, Mexican troops crossed the Rio Grande and attacked American forces. President James K. Polk used this as a justification to declare war, famously stating that American blood had been shed on American soil. Congress quickly approved the declaration, though not without opposition from some members who viewed the conflict as an unjust war of aggression.

The U.S. strategy involved a three-pronged approach:

1. A campaign into northern Mexico led by General Zachary Taylor
2. An expedition to capture Mexico City, commanded by General Winfield Scott
3. A western campaign to seize California and New Mexico, led by Colonel Stephen W. Kearny

Key Battles and Turning Points

The war saw several significant battles that demonstrated the strengths and weaknesses of both sides:

• The Battle of Palo Alto (May 8, 1846): The first major engagement, where superior U.S. artillery proved decisive.
• The Battle of Monterrey (September 21-24, 1846): A hard-fought victory for U.S. forces, capturing this key Mexican city after intense urban combat.
• The Battle of Buena Vista (February 22-23, 1847): A crucial victory for General Taylor against a larger Mexican force led by General Antonio López de Santa Anna.

• The Siege of Veracruz (March 9-29, 1847): General Scott's amphibious landing and capture of this key port city, opening the way for the march to Mexico City.
• The Battle of Chapultepec (September 12-13, 1847): The final assault on Mexico City, famously involving young military cadets defending their school.

Throughout the conflict, American forces, though often outnumbered, prevailed due to superior technology, leadership, and logistics. The war also saw the emergence of future military leaders who would play significant roles in the American Civil War, including Ulysses S. Grant, Robert E. Lee, and Jefferson Davis.

The Treaty of Guadalupe Hidalgo

After capturing Mexico City in September 1847, the U.S. negotiated the Treaty of Guadalupe Hidalgo, signed on February 2, 1848. *The treaty's main provisions included:*

1. Mexico ceding nearly half its territory to the United States, including present-day California, Nevada, Utah, and parts of Arizona, New Mexico, and Colorado. This vast area, known as the Mexican Cession, added about 525,000 square miles to U.S. territory.
2. The U.S. paying Mexico $15 million for the ceded territories and assuming $3.25 million in claims U.S. citizens had against Mexico.
3. The Rio Grande being established as the southern border of Texas.
4. Protection of property and civil rights for Mexican citizens living in the ceded territories, though these protections were often ignored in practice.

Impact and Legacy

The Mexican-American War had far-reaching consequences for both nations:

For the United States:
• Massive territorial expansion, fulfilling the vision of Manifest Destiny
• Intensified debates over the expansion of slavery into new territories, contributing to sectional tensions that would lead to the Civil War
• The rise of military leaders who would later play crucial roles in the Civil War
• Increased national confidence and a sense of continental dominance

For Mexico:
• Loss of about half its national territory
• Political instability and economic challenges that persisted for decades
• A lasting impact on Mexican-American relations and national identity
• The beginning of significant Mexican immigration to the United States

Reflection and Modern Relevance

The Mexican-American War raises important questions about national expansion, justifications for war, and the treatment of conquered peoples. As you study this conflict, consider:

• How did the war shape the modern United States, both geographically and culturally?
• What ethical questions does the concept of Manifest Destiny raise, and how do they relate to modern foreign policy?
• How has the relationship between the U.S. and Mexico evolved since the war, and what challenges remain?

Understanding the Mexican-American War is crucial for grasping the complexities of U.S. history, foreign policy, and the ongoing discussions about borders and immigration in North America.

The Mexican-American War was a defining moment in U.S. history, dramatically altering the nation's geography and setting the stage for future conflicts. Its legacy continues to influence American politics, culture, and international relations to this day.

22. The Mexican-American War
GUIDED NOTES

I. Key Terms

1. Manifest Destiny: ______________________________

2. Annexation: ______________________________

3. Treaty of Guadalupe Hidalgo: ______________________________

4. Mexican Cession: ______________________________

5. Rio Grande: ______________________________

II. Main Concept Overview

The Mexican-American War was a conflict between ________________ and ________________ that began in _______. It resulted in significant ________________ for the United States and had lasting impacts on both nations.

III. Matching Section

Match the term with its correct description:

_____ Zachary Taylor	A. U.S. President during the war
_____ James K. Polk	B. Led the expedition to capture Mexico City
_____ Winfield Scott	C. Led the northern campaign in Mexico
_____ Stephen W. Kearny	D. Mexican general who fought at Buena Vista
_____ Santa Anna	E. Led the western campaign to seize California and New Mexico

IV. Fill in the Table

Complete the table with information about key battles of the Mexican-American War:

Battle Name	Date	Significance
Palo Alto		
Buena Vista		
Veracruz		
Chapultepec		

V. True/False

______ The Mexican-American War began when Mexican troops crossed the Rio Grande and attacked American forces.

______ The Treaty of Guadalupe Hidalgo resulted in Mexico ceding nearly half its territory to the United States.

______ The war intensified debates over the expansion of slavery in the U.S.

______ General Zachary Taylor led the campaign to capture Mexico City.

______ The Mexican Cession included the present-day states of California and Nevada.

VI. Application Question

Explain how the annexation of Texas by the United States contributed to the start of the Mexican-American War.

____

____

____

VII. Reflection/Summary

Summarize the main provisions of the Treaty of Guadalupe Hidalgo. How did this treaty impact both the United States and Mexico?

____

____

____

____

22. The Mexican-American War - Reflection Questions

1

How did the concept of Manifest Destiny influence American actions leading up to and during the Mexican-American War?

How might this idea be viewed differently today? Think about the beliefs and attitudes that drove American expansion. Consider how the idea of Manifest Destiny might be perceived in today's global context. How have views on territorial expansion and national destiny changed since the 19th century?

2

In what ways did the Mexican-American War impact the debate over slavery in the United States?

How did this conflict contribute to the growing tensions that eventually led to the Civil War? Consider the new territories acquired as a result of the war. How did this acquisition reignite debates about the expansion of slavery?

3

How did the Mexican-American War shape the modern-day border between the United States and Mexico?

What long-term consequences has this had for both nations and their relationship? Reflect on the current U.S.-Mexico border and its origins in this conflict. Consider issues like immigration, cross-border relations, and cultural exchange. How have these been influenced by the war's outcome?

Scenario 1

Scenario: Diplomatic Crisis at the Border

Imagine that a diplomatic crisis erupts between the U.S. and Mexico over a disputed section of the border, reminiscent of the pre-war dispute over Texas's southern border. A U.S. border patrol team is detained by Mexican authorities who claim they crossed into Mexican territory.

a) How might this incident escalate or de-escalate based on the actions of both governments?
b) What role might international organizations like the UN play in resolving this dispute?
c) How would public opinion and media coverage influence the governments' responses?

Scenario 2

Technological Warfare and Public Opinion

Drawing a parallel to the military technology gap in the Mexican-American War, consider a scenario where the U.S. employs advanced drone technology in a border security operation, leading to international controversy.

a) How might this use of technology affect the balance of power between the two nations?
b) What ethical questions does this raise, similar to debates about the justice of the Mexican-American War?
c) How might social media and instant communication influence public opinion and governmental decision-making in this scenario?

22. The Mexican-American War - Vocabulary

TERM	DEFINITION
Annexation	
Expansion	
Guadalupe	
Hidalgo	
Nueces	

TERM	DEFINITION
Polk	
Rio Grande	
Santa Anna	
Scott	
Taylor	

The Mexican-American War

G U A D A L U P E S I X C O H Q N K A Z D Y R T

L R G P M S E N I C L V E A N W G X N K B Q R P

Q Z L G B O Y Q V A C F D Q U E X Z B D G F I O

Y F C X E P A Q C D A M G O E V F H D E R E O F

K T S O H B B H R V A X X K C Y V M K J M I G M

L P J Q I Q J M F B L A G Y E T G C O V Q C R V

L O X X Z U T D X U V D I X S N Q H K K Y G A V

F N G L E A H A T A K U J F U S X T O J N P N P

E T N W L U D F Y A N N E X A T I O N Z K B D H

C E B D V E D O R L E O N Y T B U H R W V O E G

S H B F V F C W C R O X S I N Q K I G R K Y X S

Q Y U Z E M M H P T O R P N J U B Q V N Y I B P

U O B E A C I Z C B R U J A E S V O Y S R O R J

U M V H S M S M Y S O P X B N M S Z H M T D M Q

P O L K B O D C X Y Q F N Q L S G T U D H I M M

W W N J A S R F S J U P V N M S I J A H O T S Q

L S A N T A A N N A H A K L A K E O U R B O Q C

P Y R E Y M F X W S Q D X P N H K H N J D J T H

A O V P A L A W S C O T T Y J N Q B C K B C L U

K O E S Y U Z E L Y D S D M R J P E H F K X D M

S P L X O M A N I F E S T C N U A J H E B W J W

B Q P A X U A S N J I I A S V M J G H J K E M F

F P G P Q V N S Q C Y U U H Z H V G O B Z D O F

V M T A Q P Y J E T U E H A B R Z P Q V T W G Q

Taylor

Scott

Santa Anna

Rio Grande

Polk

Nueces

Manifest

Guadalupe

Expansion

Annexation

The Mexican-American War

Across

2. Texas experienced this in 1845, triggering tensions.

3. U.S. general who led the northern campaign.

6. River established as the U.S.-Mexico border post-war. (2 words)

8. U.S. President during the Mexican-Amer War.

9. U.S. general who captured Mexico City.

10. _____ Destiny justified expansion.

Down

1. Manifest Destiny drove American territorial _____.

4. _____ Hidalgo brought peace in 1848.

5. Mexico claimed this, not the Rio Grande, as the boundary.

7. Antonio López de _____ _____ led Mexican forces.

23. The Gold Rush and Settlement of the West

by 3andB Staff Writer | October 1, 2024

Striking Gold: The Rush That Shaped the American West

Imagine a discovery so enticing it could make thousands of people drop everything and race across a continent. In 1848, that's exactly what happened when gold was found in California, setting off a chain of events that would reshape America forever. Welcome to the California Gold Rush, a pivotal chapter in the settlement of the American West.

The Gold Rush of 1849 spurred rapid westward settlement as thousands flocked to California in search of fortune, transforming the region's demographics and economy.

The Spark That Ignited a Nation

On January 24, 1848, James W. Marshall discovered gold flakes in the American River at Sutter's Mill, California. This small event would soon balloon into one of the largest migrations in American history. As news spread, a diverse wave of fortune-seekers, known as "forty-niners," flooded into California from all corners of the globe.

The Gold Rush wasn't just about finding riches – it was a catalyst for massive change, accelerating the settlement of the West and fundamentally altering the American landscape.

Gold Fever: A Nation on the Move

The journey to California was no easy feat. Aspiring miners faced three main routes:

1. The sea voyage around Cape Horn
2. The treacherous Panama shortcut
3. The overland trail across the continent

Each path presented its own set of dangers, from shipwrecks and tropical diseases to hostile encounters and harsh weather. Yet, the promise of gold proved too tempting to resist. By 1855, California's non-native population had swelled from just 14,000 to a staggering 300,000.

Beyond the Gold: Building a New Society

While many came for gold, the Rush's impact extended far beyond the mines. It spurred rapid development in California and surrounding territories:

- *Boomtowns:* Settlements like San Francisco exploded in size, transforming from sleepy villages to bustling cities almost overnight.
- *Infrastructure:* The need to support the growing population led to the quick development of roads, railroads, and communication networks.
- *Agriculture:* To feed the miners, California's fertile valleys were rapidly converted into farmland, laying the groundwork for the state's agricultural dominance.

The Gold Rush also had profound social implications. It brought together people from diverse backgrounds, creating a unique melting pot in the West. However, this rapid influx also led to conflicts with Native American tribes and discrimination against non-white miners.

The Environmental Toll

The pursuit of gold came at a significant environmental cost. New mining techniques like hydraulic mining devastated landscapes, washing away entire hillsides and clogging rivers with debris. The long-term effects of these practices would be felt for generations to come.

Legacy of the Rush

Although the Gold Rush eventually waned, its impact on American history was indelible:

1. *Statehood:* California achieved statehood in 1850, much faster than it would have otherwise.
2. *Economic Shift:* The Rush accelerated America's transition from an agricultural to an industrial economy.
3. *Cultural Identity:* The idea of the rugged, independent prospector became a key part of American mythology.

The California Gold Rush reminds us that history is often made not just by grand plans, but by the collective actions of ordinary people chasing extraordinary dreams. It's a testament to human ambition, the power of hope, and the complex consequences that can arise from our pursuit of prosperity.

The Ripple Effect

The impact of the Gold Rush extended far beyond California's borders. It accelerated the settlement of other western territories as disappointed miners spread out in search of new opportunities. The rush for resources wasn't limited to gold either – soon, silver discoveries in Nevada and Colorado sparked their own migration waves.

This rapid westward expansion also intensified conflicts with Native American tribes, leading to numerous wars and the eventual confinement of many tribes to reservations. The Gold Rush thus played a significant role in reshaping not just the physical landscape of the West, but its demographic and cultural makeup as well.

Technological Advancements

The challenges of mining in California spurred numerous technological innovations. New methods of extracting gold were developed, from simple tools like the gold pan to more complex mechanisms like the hydraulic monitor. These advancements in mining technology would have far-reaching effects, influencing industrial practices well beyond the gold fields.

A New American Dream

Perhaps the most enduring legacy of the Gold Rush was how it shaped the American psyche. The idea that one could strike it rich through luck and hard work became deeply ingrained in the national consciousness. This "rags to riches" narrative, while not always reflecting reality, became a cornerstone of the American Dream.

Did You Know?

• The largest gold nugget found during the California Gold Rush weighed 195 pounds!
• The term "Eureka!" (Greek for "I have found it!") became California's official state motto due to the Gold Rush.

As you reflect on the Gold Rush, consider how a single discovery can set off a chain reaction that reshapes a nation. What modern events might have a similar transformative power? How might our actions today create ripple effects that future generations will study?

The California Gold Rush stands as a testament to the power of human ambition and the complex interplay between opportunity, migration, and societal change. Its effects, both positive and negative, continue to shape the American West and the nation as a whole to this day.

23. The Gold Rush and Settlement of the West

GUIDED NOTES

I. Key Terms

1. Gold Rush: ____
2. Forty-niners: ____
3. Boomtowns: ____
4. Statehood: ____

II. Main Concept Overview

The California Gold Rush was a significant event that ____________________ the settlement of the American West. It began in __________ when James W. Marshall discovered ______________ at Sutter's Mill, California.

III. Matching Section

Match the term with its correct description:

_____ 1. Cape Horn	A. Shortcut route through Central America
_____ 2. Panama	B. Southernmost tip of South America
_____ 3. Overland trail	C. Route across the North American continent
_____ 4. San Francisco	D. Major boomtown of the Gold Rush
_____ 5. Native Americans	E. Indigenous peoples affected by westward expansion

IV. Fill in the Table

Complete the table with information about the impacts of the Gold Rush:

Area of Impact	Description of Impact
Population	
Infrastructure	
Agriculture	
Environment	
Economy	

V. True/False

_____ The California Gold Rush had little impact on America's transition from an agricultural to an industrial economy.

_____ The Gold Rush led to the rapid development of roads, railroads, and communication networks in the West.

_____ The environmental impact of the Gold Rush was minimal and short-lived.

_____ California achieved statehood in 1850, partly due to the rapid population growth caused by the Gold Rush.

_____ The Gold Rush only attracted people from within the United States.

VI. Application Question

Describe how the California Gold Rush might have affected a Native American tribe living in California during that time. Consider both short-term and long-term impacts.

____

____

____

VII. Reflection/Summary

In your own words, summarize the main impacts of the California Gold Rush on the settlement of the American West. How does this historical event relate to the concept of the "American Dream"?

____

____

____

____

23. The Gold Rush and Settlement of the West - Reflection Questions

1

How might your life be different if you suddenly discovered a gold mine on your property today?

What opportunities and challenges would you face? Consider how sudden wealth might change your daily life, relationships, and future plans. Think about the potential positive and negative consequences of such a discovery.

2

In what ways do you think the Gold Rush experience shaped the concept of the "American Dream"?

How does this historical event relate to modern ideas of success and opportunity? Reflect on the "rags to riches" narrative associated with the Gold Rush. Consider how this event might have influenced American values and beliefs about success and opportunity that persist today.

3

Compare the Gold Rush's impact to modern resource booms. What similarities and differences do you see?

Think about current examples of resource booms (e.g., oil, rare earth minerals). Consider the similarities and differences in terms of economic impact, environmental concerns, and societal changes.

23. The Gold Rush and Settlement of the West - Hypotheticals

Scenario 1

Scenario: Imagine that a new, revolutionary battery technology is discovered in a small town in Nevada, promising to make electric vehicles cheaper and more efficient than gas-powered cars.

a) How might this discovery affect migration patterns within the United States?
b) What economic and environmental impacts might this have on Nevada and surrounding states?
c) How could this technology change the global balance of power in the automotive and energy industries?

Scenario 2

Scenario: What if a private company discovers a way to efficiently extract rare earth minerals from the ocean floor, but the process poses potential risks to marine ecosystems?

a) How might different stakeholders (government, environmentalists, tech companies) react to this discovery?
b) What kind of regulations might be put in place, and how could they affect the development of this new industry?
c) How might this discovery impact global trade relationships, particularly with countries that currently dominate rare earth mineral production?

23. The Gold Rush and Settlement of the West - Vocabulary

TERM	DEFINITION
Gold Rush	
Forty-niners	
Boomtown	
Sutter's Mill	
Hydraulic mining	

TERM	DEFINITION
Prospector	
Statehood	
Infrastructure	
Melting pot	
American Dream	

The Gold Rush and Settlement of the West

```
K P S U T T E R S M I L L A J M L H X D C A H Y
D P T K K S R T U K P I Z E R R R B U U X F O D
X L M I Q P P H D L S U J C S E U J A O P P H C
U N Y C N H A Y B M W R B G N I Q M Z E Z L S S
S R X S Z F B D C G C T I D J W A P I Z R H K M
F E V Q R L R R R O U B D L E H P X C O P J Y J
M B M F P Z S A A J P E I X X G O V L R A Z E B
D K U E D H A U S L C L I A W H N W S X X A I H
D G A W D Y M L K T I S W R J B B X O S T Z Z B
S R S W Y H E I W B R H F F O R T Y N I N E R S
S S T U M C R C V H O U K Z J C S S C P K O Z N
P T I L X P I M D Z H O C K X I O M T R U K A D
N A C M P B C I Y M H X M T P T J C Q H P L V K
U T T I N M A N D U F H I T U K C X N H R F M F
D E Y X W P N I Z Y R J Y V O R O J O I O M H E
F H F E I O D N P U C O M N J W E B F U S H J J
E O V G M W R G O W J G K B J O N C B W P V W B
W O A Q H E E Y A U T J I J K A E C D G E H G Q
X D W T K F A F C D V E N M B W Q O A U C W I J
E U S K R Y M I N B N M E L T I N G P O T J H W
N D G O L D R U S H I Z X Z K Y R Q U M O U N N
Q E R D E F U D A N Y D J U R I F C M Y R C I S
A I F M J Y G Y S O N F Y Q R A S I Z H Z U K M
M Z T U Y N F M J N H Y J Z F Y D K S C W C N K
```

American Dream

Statehood

Sutter's Mill

Gold Rush

Melting pot

Prospector

Boomtown

Infrastructure

Hydraulic mining

Forty-niners

The Gold Rush and Settlement of the West

Across

4. One who seeks fortune with a pan and a dream.

6. Roads, rails, and wires that grew as fast as the population.

7. Cultural mixture stirred up by the Rush. (2 words)

8. Rags-to-riches notion fueled by golden hopes. (2 words)

9. A settlement that grows faster than Jack's beanstalk.

10. Water-powered technique that washed away more than just dirt. (2-words)

Down

1. Treasure seekers who weren't NFL players. (2-words)

2. Sudden migration sparked by a glittering discovery. (2 words)

3. California's new status, achieved in record time.

5. California site where the sparkly saga began. (2 words)

by 3andB Staff Writer | October 1, 2024

The Wheels of Progress: Technological Advancements and the Market Revolution

In the early 19th century, America experienced a profound transformation that would reshape its economy, society, and very landscape. This period, known as the Market Revolution, was driven by technological advancements that revolutionized transportation, communication, and production. Let's explore how these innovations propelled the United States into a new era of economic growth and social change.

The Steam-Powered Revolution

At the heart of this transformation was the steam engine. This powerful invention breathed life into new forms of transportation and manufacturing, fundamentally altering the way Americans lived and worked.

Technological advancements like the telegraph and steam engine during the Market Revolution transformed communication and transportation, driving 19th-century economic growth.

Steamboats: Rivers of Opportunity

Robert Fulton's successful demonstration of the steamboat in 1807 marked the beginning of a new age in water transportation. Steamboats could travel upstream with ease, dramatically reducing travel times and transportation costs. The Mississippi River and its tributaries became bustling highways of commerce, connecting the frontier to eastern markets and accelerating westward expansion.

Railways: Tying the Nation Together

The development of steam-powered locomotives and the expansion of railway networks had an even more profound impact. By the 1850s, over 30,000 miles of track crisscrossed the nation, connecting cities, farms, and factories. This vast network allowed for the rapid and efficient movement of goods and people, stimulating economic growth and national unity.

Communication Revolution: The Telegraph

While steam power revolutionized physical transportation, the invention of the telegraph by Samuel Morse in 1844 transformed the speed of communication. Messages that once took weeks to deliver could now be transmitted almost instantly across great distances. This technological marvel facilitated faster business transactions, improved coordination of railway traffic, and even changed the nature of journalism and warfare.

The Rise of Factory Production

Technological advancements also dramatically altered the way goods were produced. The development of interchangeable parts and the adoption of the assembly line led to the rise of factory production. This shift from artisanal to industrial manufacturing increased productivity and lowered costs, making a wide range of goods more affordable and accessible to average Americans.

The Textile Industry: A Case Study

Nowhere was this change more evident than in the textile industry. Innovations like the power loom and the cotton gin revolutionized cloth production. Northern textile mills, particularly in New England, became centers of industrial growth, while Southern cotton plantations expanded to meet the increasing demand for raw materials.

The Market Revolution: A New Economic Order

These technological advancements fueled what historians call the Market Revolution – a shift from local, largely self-sufficient economies to a more interconnected, specialized, and market-oriented system.

Specialization and Interdependence

As transportation and communication improved, regions began to specialize in particular products. The Northeast focused on manufacturing, the South on cotton production, and the Midwest on grain farming. This specialization increased efficiency but also made different regions more economically interdependent.

The Rise of Wage Labor

The growth of factories and urban centers led to a fundamental shift in labor relations. Many Americans moved from being self-employed farmers or artisans to wage laborers in factories or on commercial farms. This change had profound social implications, altering traditional work rhythms and family structures.

Expanding Markets

Improved transportation and communication networks allowed businesses to reach wider markets. Local shopkeepers were increasingly replaced by larger merchants who could take advantage of these new opportunities. The result was the emergence of a more dynamic and competitive commercial environment.

Social and Cultural Impact

The Market Revolution wasn't just an economic phenomenon – it reshaped American society and culture in significant ways:

1. Urbanization: As factories grew, so did cities, leading to rapid urbanization, particularly in the North.
2. Immigration: Economic opportunities attracted waves of immigrants, particularly from Europe, changing the nation's demographic makeup.
3. Reform Movements: The social disruptions caused by these changes sparked various reform movements, addressing issues like workers' rights, temperance, and women's suffrage.

The technological advancements and the resulting Market Revolution of the early 19th century laid the foundation for the United States to become an industrial and economic powerhouse. This period of rapid change brought both opportunities and challenges, shaping the nation in ways that continue to influence American life today. As we reflect on this transformative era, we can see the roots of many contemporary issues, from economic inequality to technological disruption, reminding us that understanding our past is key to navigating our future.

24. Technological Advancements and the Market Revolution

GUIDED NOTES

I. Key Terms

1. Market Revolution: ____

2. Steam Engine: ____

3. Telegraph: ____

4. Interchangeable Parts: ____

5. Power Loom: ____

II. Main Concept Overview

The early 19th century in America was marked by significant ________________ advancements that led to a profound economic transformation known as the ________________ Revolution. This period saw dramatic changes in ________________, ________________, and production methods.

III. Matching Section

Match the term with its correct description:

_____ Steamboat	A. Invented by Samuel Morse in 1844
_____ Railway	B. Facilitated faster business transactions
_____ Telegraph	C. Revolutionized river transportation
_____ Cotton Gin	D. Connected cities across the nation
_____ Power Loom	E. Revolutionized cloth production

IV. True/False

______ The Market Revolution led to increased regional specialization.

______ Steamboats primarily traveled on the Mississippi River and its tributaries.

______ The telegraph had no significant impact on journalism or warfare.

______ The rise of factories led to a shift from self-employment to wage labor.

______ The Market Revolution contributed to increased urbanization, particularly in the North.

V. Application Question

Imagine you are a farmer in the Midwest in the 1850s. How might the technological advancements and economic changes of the Market Revolution affect your farming practices and lifestyle? Provide at least three specific examples based on the information in the article.

____

____

____

____

VI. Reflection/Summary

Summarize the main impacts of the Market Revolution on American society and economy. How do you think these changes might have set the stage for future developments in the United States?

____

____

____

____

____

1

How do you think your daily life would be different if you lived during the Market Revolution?

Consider aspects such as communication, transportation, and the goods you use. Think about the technologies you rely on every day. How would the absence of instant communication or rapid transportation affect your routines and relationships? Consider how access to goods and services might be different.

2

In what ways do you see parallels between the Market Revolution and the current digital revolution?

Consider how the internet and digital technologies have changed the way we work, communicate, and conduct business. Are there similarities in terms of economic specialization, market reach, or social impacts?

3

The article mentions that understanding this period helps us navigate contemporary issues.

Can you identify a current societal or economic challenge that has roots in the Market Revolution era? Think about ongoing debates about workers' rights, economic inequality, or the impact of technological change. How might these issues be connected to the transformations that occurred during the Market Revolution?

Scenario 1

Scenario: What if smartphones had never been invented?

Imagine that instead of smartphones, we still used basic cell phones that could only make calls and send text messages. Tablets and laptops are still available, but there's no all-in-one mobile device.

a) How would this change the way you communicate with friends and family?
b) How might this affect businesses that rely on mobile apps, like ride-sharing or food delivery services?
c) What might be some positive and negative effects on society if smartphones didn't exist?

Scenario 2

Scenario: What if a new technology allowed students to download knowledge directly to their brains?

Suppose a safe, affordable device was invented that could transfer information directly into your memory. Instead of studying, you could download facts and skills instantly.

a) How might this change your school experience and the way you learn?
b) What potential benefits and drawbacks can you see from this technology?
c) How might this affect future job prospects and the value of different skills in the workforce?

24. Technological Advancements and the Market Revolution - Vocabulary

TERM	DEFINITION
Assembly Line	
Factory	
Industrial	
Locomotive	
Market Revolution	

TERM	DEFINITION
Power Loom	
Railroad	
Specialization	
Steam Engine	
Telegraph	

Technological Advancements and the Market Revolution

M L X V H E W U A W L S I S M E H Z F X O H X P
C F A J Q T Y J H Y O L Q U G V X J M Z E D F Y
S Q E H S T M J U P C R I L S Q J U V K Z H C Q
P Y F G Q R F Y Z U O R N B O V Q K O D E K F N
E Q C A W S W D H Z M E D K B Z V V I B K D C C
C B Q Z C M H V G I O W U X I G O R E X F A F T
I T L T J T J R W X T A S Q Z E H B W L U S M A
A G G E A V O Q K A I F T T T I Z F T R K S G H
L V A L C D A R F R V J R D J M B A V N E E D D
I A E E E O O Z Y F E T I V P F J M P P L M N E
Z D Q G Q I P S Y R E W A R G A H H R W S B P M
A L I R G K X O C Q M T L F E R T F Q B S L U Q
T Y W A Q I U I W G H X I F H X P H Q A L Y Q E
I W E P C S F P P E K I E D O C Z G T V G L P O
O V C H E E U Q M A R K E T R E V O L U T I O N
N G H H Q H X Z C X Y L V I C M F F K X D N I R
B J L P L V D H V L P E O N W R O G M A D E Z H
T L P C O A N H T J S B M O R A I L R O A D Z Q
A R M G Z J I Q Z P F Y T F M Q D B Y D S H J C
R R A H R J B P Q H T Z D A Q G O P C V R Q A U
O C X B S B C B N T Q D G T M C R S F F M C W W
M K V T N N N H H Q C G C F L I Y E X S S W I Q
B A L V S T E A M E N G I N E P Q B N K M V O J
Z E M R U X W C V T C W O W J T F E K W O D J X

Telegraph
Railroad
Locomotive
Assembly Line

Steam Engine
Power Loom
Industrial

Specialization
Market Revolution
Factory

Technological Advancements and the Market Revolution

Across

2. Related to large-scale manufacturing and production.

4. Machine that automated cloth weaving. (2 words)

7. Steam-powered engine that pulled trains.

9. Network of tracks that connected cities and regions.

10. Period of economic transformation in early 19th century America. (2 words)

Down

1. Factory innovation that sped up production. (2 words)

3. Focus on producing specific goods or services.

5. Center of industrial production in the Market Revolution.

6. Invention that powered the Industrial Revolution. (2 words)

8. Communication device that sent messages over long distances.

25. Growing Sectional Tensions and Compromise of 1850

by 3andB Staff Writer | October 1, 2024

The Path to Compromise: Growing Sectional Tensions and the Compromise of 1850

As the United States expanded westward in the mid-19th century, a storm was brewing. The question of slavery's expansion into new territories threatened to tear the nation apart. This article explores the growing sectional tensions between the North and South, culminating in the Compromise of 1850—a pivotal moment that temporarily held the Union together.

The Roots of Conflict

The concept of Manifest Destiny—the belief that American expansion across the continent was both inevitable and justified—drove the nation's growth. This ideology, popularized in the 1840s, inspired Americans to push westward, leading to the acquisition of vast new territories. However, this expansion brought with it a critical question: Would new states be free or slave?

The Compromise of 1850 emerged amid growing sectional tensions over slavery, attempting to balance the interests of free and slave states.

The Missouri Compromise of 1820

This earlier compromise had maintained a delicate balance between free and slave states. It prohibited slavery north of the 36°30' parallel in the Louisiana Territory, with the exception of Missouri. For three decades, this agreement kept the peace, but westward expansion would soon challenge its effectiveness.

Flashpoints of Tension:

The Mexican-American War (1846-1848)

The war with Mexico, driven partly by the ideals of Manifest Destiny, resulted in vast new territories for the United States. The Treaty of Guadalupe Hidalgo in 1848 added more than 500,000 square miles to the nation, including parts of present-day Arizona, California, New Mexico, Texas, Colorado, Nevada, and Utah. However, it reignited the debate over slavery's expansion. Would these new lands be open to slavery or remain free?

The Wilmot Proviso

In 1846, Congressman David Wilmot of Pennsylvania proposed an amendment prohibiting slavery in any territory acquired from Mexico. The Wilmot Proviso passed in the House of Representatives, where the more populous North held a majority, but was repeatedly rejected in the Senate, where the balance between free and slave states was equal. This legislative battle highlighted the deepening divide between North and South.

The Road to Compromise: California's Gold Rush and Statehood Application

The discovery of gold in California in 1848 led to a massive population boom known as the Gold Rush. Thousands of settlers poured into the territory, rapidly increasing its population. By 1850, California had enough residents to apply for statehood—but would it be admitted as a free or slave state? As a free state, it would upset the delicate balance in the Senate, giving free states a majority and potentially tipping the scales of national power.

The Compromise of 1850

Senator Henry Clay of Kentucky, known as "The Great Compromiser" for his role in crafting earlier agreements like the Missouri Compromise, stepped forward once again. In January 1850, the 72-year-old Clay proposed a series of resolutions to address the growing crisis. These resolutions formed the basis of what would become the Compromise of 1850.

After months of heated debate and with the crucial help of Senator Stephen Douglas of Illinois, a compromise was finally reached. The Compromise of 1850 was not a single act, but a series of five separate bills passed in September 1850.

Key provisions of the Compromise of 1850 included:

1. California admitted as a free state
2. New Mexico and Utah territories organized without mention of slavery (popular sovereignty)
3. Texas's borders adjusted in exchange for federal assumption of its debt
4. A stronger Fugitive Slave Law
5. Slave trade (but not slavery) banned in Washington D.C.

Impact and Aftermath

The Compromise of 1850 temporarily eased tensions, but it was far from a permanent solution. Each side had to accept difficult concessions. The stronger Fugitive Slave Law, which required Northern states to return escaped slaves and imposed penalties on those who aided them, angered many Northerners and intensified abolitionist sentiment. Meanwhile, the concept of popular sovereignty in new territories worried Southerners, who feared it might lead to more free states in the future.

A Brief Respite

For a few years, the compromise seemed to work. Both North and South claimed victory, and the immediate threat of secession subsided. However, the underlying issues remained unresolved. The balance between free and slave states continued to be a source of tension, and the debate over slavery's morality and economic impact persisted.

Seeds of Future Conflict

While the Compromise of 1850 prevented an immediate crisis, it set the stage for future conflicts. The Kansas-Nebraska Act of 1854, which applied popular sovereignty to those territories, would soon reignite the debate over slavery's expansion. This led to violent confrontations in "Bleeding Kansas" and further escalated tensions between North and South. The Compromise of 1850 also contributed to the decline of the Whig Party and the rise of the Republican Party, reshaping the political landscape of the 1850s.

The Compromise of 1850 represents a critical moment in American history—a last-ditch effort to hold the Union together in the face of growing sectional tensions. While it succeeded in the short term, it ultimately failed to resolve the fundamental issues dividing the nation. The compromise demonstrated both the possibility of political negotiation and its limitations in addressing deep-seated moral and economic disagreements. Understanding this period is crucial for comprehending the events that would lead to the Civil War just a decade later, as well as the ongoing struggles to address issues of equality and justice in American society.

25. Growing Sectional Tensions and Compromise of 1850

GUIDED NOTES

I. Key Terms

1. Manifest Destiny: ____________________
2. Missouri Compromise: ____________________
3. Wilmot Proviso: ____________________
4. Popular Sovereignty: ____________________
5. Fugitive Slave Law: ____________________

II. Main Concept Overview

The period leading up to the Compromise of 1850 was marked by ____________________ between the North and South, primarily over the issue of ____________________ in new territories.

III. Matching Section

Match each term with its correct description:

_____ 1. Henry Clay	A. Proposed amendment prohibiting slavery in territory from Mexico
_____ 2. David Wilmot	B. Helped reach the Compromise of 1850
_____ 3. Stephen Douglas	C. Known as "The Great Compromiser"
_____ 4. California	D. Territories organized without mention of slavery in 1850
_____ 5. New Mexico/Utah	E. Applied for statehood following the Gold Rush

IV. Fill in the Table

Complete the table with the key provisions of the Compromise of 1850:

Provision	Details
California	
New Mexico and Utah Territories	
Texas	
Fugitive Slave Law	
Washington D.C.	

V. True or False

______ 1. The Missouri Compromise of 1820 maintained a balance between free and slave states for three decades.

______ 2. The Mexican-American War resulted in no new territories for the United States.

______ 3. The Wilmot Proviso passed in the House of Representatives but was rejected in the Senate.

______ 4. The Compromise of 1850 was a single act passed by Congress.

______ 5. The Kansas-Nebraska Act of 1854 applied popular sovereignty to those territories.

VI. Short Answer

1. Explain how the concept of Manifest Destiny led to the critical question about new states:

____

____

2. Describe two impacts of the Compromise of 1850 mentioned in the article:

____

____

VII. Application Question

According to the article, how did the Compromise of 1850 affect both Northern and Southern interests? Consider the Fugitive Slave Law and the concept of popular sovereignty.

____

____

VIII. Reflection/Summary

Summarize the main points of the article in your own words. How did the Compromise of 1850 both ease tensions and set the stage for future conflicts?

____

____

____

25. Growing Sectional Tensions and Compromise of 1850 - Reflection Questions

1

How might popular sovereignty have changed westward expansion?

Think about how it could have affected the balance of power between free and slave states. Consider the potential for increased conflict or cooperation among settlers with different views on slavery. Reflect on how it might have impacted the speed and pattern of territorial settlement.

2

What did the Compromise of 1850 reveal about the American political system?

Examine how the compromise demonstrated the ability to negotiate complex issues. Think about the limitations of political solutions to moral and economic disagreements. Consider the role of individual leaders like Henry Clay and Stephen Douglas in shaping the compromise.

3

How did the Fugitive Slave Law affect Northern attitudes about slavery?

Explore the personal and moral dilemmas this law created for Northerners. Think about its impact on the abolitionist movement and how it might have galvanized opposition to slavery. Consider the changes in public opinion and political discourse surrounding slavery after the law's passage.

25. Growing Sectional Tensions and Compromise of 1850 - Hypotheticals

Scenario 1

Scenario:The Green Energy Divide

Imagine that a new federal law is proposed requiring all states to derive 50% of their energy from renewable sources within 10 years. However, states with economies heavily dependent on fossil fuel industries strongly oppose this legislation.

a)How might this situation mirror the sectional tensions of the 1850s?
b)What kind of compromise could be reached to address both environmental concerns and economic interests?
c)How might this affect the balance of power between federal and state governments?

Scenario 2

Scenario: The Universal Basic Income Experiment

Imagine that in response to growing wealth inequality and job displacement due to automation, a group of states decides to implement a Universal Basic Income (UBI) program. This creates tension with states that oppose such measures.

a) What key points from the article would you emphasize in your videos?
b) How would you connect historical events to issues that teenagers care about today?
c) What creative approaches could you use to make US history more appealing to a young audience?

25. Growing Sectional Tensions and Compromise of 1850 - Vocabulary

TERM	DEFINITION
Abolitionists	
Compromise	
Expansion	
Fugitive	
Missouri Compromise	

25. Growing Sectional Tensions and Compromise of 1850 - Vocabulary

TERM	DEFINITION
Popular Sovereignty	
Proviso	
Sectional	
Slave state	
Tensions	

25: WORD SEARCH

Growing Sectional Tensions and the Compromise of 1850

N Z J U D Y N X A E K S A C L M X P A G C A P K

T W Q A V W Z U H V B A U M N O E G V U H Y V T

S K O D B V Z F L M U O V S E C T I O N A L B U

R J I J N Q E U M P N X U Y Z Q A P Y M N G N R

S U G Z O A N Z Z M B P O I Z O Y S U O X D X M

U P D U I O X B J L F S W A J G G V Z Z J M G F

I D X F G C K Q X J P M L Y T V V J V A L T D Q

P C C U N P M I S S O U R I C O M P R O M I S E

S Z O K I Y C H I K P K P T P J E T F U K F J G

P X C M Q L M U K K U E M Q S L A V E S T A T E

J B Z R P U T X S X L K X F E A E A Q G Y I B V

K A U V N R P S L Y A N L P U T U P U C K F S R

M B R Z M K O W B W R I A I A G R Q I S P F T N

M O I V U N F M T W S Z F U K N I V K L C S I L

A L Z N T D L D I Y O G R L F K S T Q N K C W E

T I E B T K K M C S V E D S Q C R I I T P X F Y

G T O D I E Q N V M E G J B E D I S O V J Z Y C

W I T E N S I O N S R T F Y I X H P L N E G H J

M O R R H T M P F G E B F R F T X M E U H V A H

Z N B E Q E F G B C I P R O V I S O E A G B I E

H I J Y F Y I B P W G Q B G L U X D W B S I G K

B S K J Y C T D J P N Z R S J Q F K Z Y O E R D

D T E R V E K H C H T I P A Z X I N N E B G W I

G S Y P U D N N Q A Y C M A J L V Q S X Q S Z P

Missoui Compromise

Popular Sovereignty

Tensions

Slave state

Sectional

Proviso

Fugitive

Expansion

Compromise

Abolitionists

Growing Sectional Tensions and the Compromise of 1850

Across

2. An 1820 agreement that maintained equilibrium between opposing forces for decades. _____ Compromise

5. Relating to distinct regions, often with conflicting interests.

6. The process of growth that brought new territories into the American fold.

7. The art of finding middle ground, as demonstrated by Clay's 1850 solution.

9. A runaway, particularly relevant to those escaping bondage in the South.

10. The principle allowing settlers to determine their territory's stance on a contentious issue, Popular _____

Down

1. Activists who fought to end the practice of owning humans as property.

3. A territory where the ownership of humans was legally permitted. (2 words)

4. Strained relations, particularly evident between North and South in the mid-19th century.

8. A condition or stipulation, like the one Wilmot proposed for newly acquired lands.

Your greatest superpower is your ability to choose one thought over another.

Choose positive thoughts over negative to live your very best life.

Our Lessons On:

TeachersPayTeachers (TPT)

https://www.teacherspayteachers.com/store/3andb

Our Workbooks On:

Amazon

https://amzn.to/3ygpsvk

Made in the USA
Middletown, DE
24 October 2024